DEPARTMENT OF THE TREASURY TECHNICAL EXPLANATION OF THE
CONVENTION BETWEEN THE GOVERNMENT OF THE UNITED STATES OF
AMERICA AND THE GOVERNMENT OF JAPAN FOR THE AVOIDANCE OF DOUBLE
TAXATION AND THE PREVENTION OF FISCAL EVASION WITH RESPECT TO
TAXES ON INCOME AND ON CAPITAL GAINS, SIGNED AT WASHINGTON
ON NOVEMBER 6, 2003

DEPARTMENT OF THE TREASURY TECHNICAL EXPLANATION OF THE
CONVENTION BETWEEN THE GOVERNMENT OF THE UNITED STATES OF
AMERICA AND THE GOVERNMENT OF JAPAN FOR THE AVOIDANCE OF DOUBLE
TAXATION AND THE PREVENTION OF FISCAL EVASION WITH RESPECT TO
TAXES ON INCOME AND ON CAPITAL GAINS, SIGNED AT WASHINGTON
ON NOVEMBER 6, 2003

This is a technical explanation of the Convention between the Government of the United States of America and the Government of Japan for the Avoidance of Double Taxation and the Prevention of Fiscal Evasion with respect to Taxes on Income, signed at Washington on November 6, 2003 (the "Convention"), and the Protocol also signed at Washington on November 6, 2003, which forms an integral part thereto (the "Protocol"). In connection with the negotiation of the Convention, the delegations of the United States and Japan developed and agreed upon an exchange of Diplomatic Notes (the "Notes"). The Notes constitute an agreement between the two governments that shall enter into force at the same time as the entry into force of the Convention. The Notes are intended to give guidance both to the taxpayers and to the tax authorities of the Contracting States in interpreting the Convention. The Notes and Protocol are discussed below in connection with relevant provisions of the Convention.

References are made to the Convention between the Government of the United States of America and the Government of Japan for the Avoidance of Double Taxation and the Prevention of Fiscal Evasion with respect to Taxes on Income, signed at Tokyo on March 8, 1971 (the "prior Convention"). The Convention and Protocol replace the prior Convention.

Negotiations took into account the U.S. Treasury Department's current tax treaty policy and the Treasury Department's Model Income Tax Convention, published on September 20, 1996 (the "U.S. Model"). Negotiations also took into account the Model Tax Convention on Income and on Capital, published by the Organization for Economic Cooperation and Development, as updated in January 2003 (the "OECD Model"), and recent tax treaties concluded by both countries.

The Technical Explanation is an official guide to the Convention. It reflects the policies behind particular Convention provisions, as well as understandings reached with respect to the application and interpretation of the Convention. While the Convention does not include subject matter headings or titles for the Articles, such headings are included in the Technical Explanation for ease of use. The headings included generally correspond to headings of analogous articles of the U.S. Model where possible, and it is not intended that any legal effect be given to the headings or to the fact of their inclusion in the Technical Explanation. References in the Technical Explanation to "he" or "his" should be read to mean "he or she" or "his or her."

Article 1 (General Scope)

Paragraph 1

Paragraph 1 of Article 1 provides that the Convention applies to residents of the United States or Japan, except where the terms of the Convention provide otherwise. Under Article 4 (Residence), a person is generally treated as a resident of a Contracting State if that person is, under the laws of that Contracting State, liable to tax therein by reason of his domicile, residence, citizenship, place of head or main office, place or incorporation, or other similar criteria. However, if a person is considered a resident of both Contracting States, Article 4 provides rules for determining a single Contracting State of residence (or no Contracting State of residence). This determination generally governs for purposes of the Convention.

Certain provisions are applicable to persons who may not be residents of either Contracting State. For example, Article 18 (Government Service) may apply to an employee of a Contracting State who is resident in neither Contracting State. Under Article 26 (Exchange of Information), information may be exchanged with respect to residents of third states.

Paragraph 2

Paragraph 2 states the generally accepted relationship both between the Convention and the domestic law of the Contracting States and between the Convention and other agreements between the Contracting States: that no provision of the Convention may restrict any benefit accorded by the tax laws of the Contracting States or by any other bilateral agreement between the Contracting States or any multilateral agreement to which the Contracting States are parties. The relationship between the non-discrimination provisions of the Convention and other agreements is addressed not in paragraph 2 but in paragraph 3.

Under paragraph 2, for example, if a deduction would be allowed under the U.S. Internal Revenue Code (the "Code") in computing the U.S. taxable income of a resident of Japan, the deduction also is allowed to that person in computing taxable income under the Convention. Paragraph 2 also means that the Convention may not increase the tax burden on a resident of a Contracting State beyond the burden determined under domestic law. Thus, a right to tax given by the Convention cannot be exercised unless that right also exists under internal law.

It follows that, under the principle of paragraph 2, a taxpayer's U.S. tax liability need not be determined under the Convention if the Code would produce a more favorable result. A taxpayer may not, however, choose among the provisions of the Code and the Convention in an inconsistent manner in order to minimize tax. For example, assume that a resident of Japan has three separate businesses in the United States. One is a profitable permanent establishment and the other two are trades or businesses that would earn taxable income under the Code but that do not meet the permanent establishment threshold tests of the Convention. One is profitable and the other incurs a loss. Under the Convention, the income of the permanent establishment is taxable in the United States, and both the profit and loss of the other two businesses are ignored. Under the Code, all three would be subject to tax, but the loss would offset the profits of the two profitable ventures. The taxpayer may not invoke the Convention to exclude the profit of the profitable trade or business and invoke the Code to claim the loss of the losing trade or business against the profit of the permanent establishment. *See* Rev. Rul. 84-17, 1984-1 C.B. 308. If, however, the taxpayer invokes the Code for the taxation of all three ventures, the taxpayer would not be precluded from invoking the Convention, for example, with respect to any dividend income the taxpayer may receive from the United States that is not effectively connected with any of the taxpayer's business activities in the United States.

Similarly, nothing in the Convention can be used to deny any benefit granted by any other agreement between the United States and Japan. For example, if certain benefits are provided for military personnel or military contractors under a status of forces agreement between the United States and Japan, those benefits will be available to residents of the Contracting States regardless of any provisions to the contrary (or silence) in the Convention.

Paragraph 3

Paragraph 3 specifically relates to the application to the Convention of dispute-resolution procedures and non-discrimination provisions under other agreements. The provisions of paragraph 3 are an exception to the rule provided in subparagraph (b) of paragraph 2 under which the Convention shall not restrict in any manner any benefit now or hereafter accorded by any other agreement between the Contracting States.

Clause (i) of subparagraph (a) of paragraph 3 provides that, notwithstanding any other agreement to which the Contracting States may be parties, a dispute concerning the interpretation or application of the Convention, including a dispute concerning whether a measure is within the scope of the Convention, shall be considered only by the competent authorities of the Contracting States, and the procedures under Article 25 of the Convention exclusively shall apply to the dispute. Thus, dispute-resolution procedures that may be incorporated into trade, investment, or other agreements between the Contracting States shall not apply in determining the scope of the Convention.

Clause (ii) of subparagraph (a) of paragraph 3 provides that the national treatment provision in Article XVII of the General Agreement on Trade in Services ("GATS") shall not apply to any "measure" unless the competent authorities agree that such measure is not within the scope of the non-discrimination provisions of Article 24 (Non-Discrimination) of the Convention. Subparagraph (b) of paragraph 3 defines the term "measure" to mean a law, regulation, rule, procedure, decision, administrative action, or any similar provision or action, as related to taxes of every kind and description imposed by a Contracting State. Accordingly, no national treatment obligation undertaken by a Contracting State pursuant to GATS shall apply to a measure, unless the competent authorities otherwise agree. The Convention does not provide any limitation on the application of the most favored nation obligation ("MFN") of Article II of GATS. Because there is no MFN obligation in the Convention, there can be no conflict between the Convention and the MFN obligation of GATS.

The Convention does not include additional limitations in the U.S. Model on the application of the national treatment and MFN obligations of other agreements. The U.S. Model provision states generally that national treatment or MFN obligations undertaken by the

Contracting States under any agreement other than the tax treaty and the General Agreement on Tariffs and Trade as applicable to trade in goods do not apply to a taxation measure, unless the competent authorities otherwise agree. Except as discussed above with respect to GATS, subparagraph 2(b) of the Convention provides that if there were overlap between Article 24 of the Convention and the national treatment or MFN obligations of any agreement, benefits would be available under both the Convention and that agreement. In the event of such overlap, to the extent benefits are available under that agreement that are not available under Article 24 of the Convention, a resident of a Contracting State is entitled to the benefits provided under the overlapping agreement.

Paragraph 4

Subparagraph (a) of paragraph 4 contains the traditional saving clause found in U.S. tax treaties. The Contracting States reserve their rights, except as provided in paragraph 5, to tax their residents and, in the case of the United States, its citizens, as provided in their internal laws, notwithstanding any provisions of the Convention to the contrary. For example, if a resident of Japan performs professional services in the United States and the income from the services is not attributable to a permanent establishment in the United States, Article 7 would by its terms prevent the United States from taxing the income. If, however, the resident of Japan is also a citizen of the United States, the saving clause permits the United States to include the remuneration in the worldwide income of the citizen and subject it to tax under the normal Code rules without regard to Code section 894(a). However, subparagraph 5 of this Article preserves the benefits of special foreign tax credit rules applicable to the U.S. taxation of certain U.S. income of its citizens resident in Japan. See paragraph 3 of Article 23 (Relief from Double Taxation).

For purposes of the saving clause, "residence" is determined under Article 4 (Residence). Thus, an individual who is a U.S. resident under the Internal Revenue Code but who is deemed to be a resident of Japan under the tie-breaker rules of Article 4 would be subject to U.S. tax only to the extent permitted by the Convention. For example, if an individual who is not a U.S. citizen is a resident of the United States under the Code, and is also a resident of Japan under its law, and that individual has a permanent home available to him in Japan and not in the United States, he would be treated as a resident of Japan under Article 4 and for purposes of the saving clause. Under the Convention, that individual would not be subject to taxation by the United States under the normal Code rules.

However, the person would be considered a U.S. resident for U.S. tax purposes other than determining the individual's U.S. tax liability. For example, in determining under Code section 957 whether a foreign corporation is a controlled foreign corporation, shares in that corporation held by the individual would be considered to be held by a U.S. resident. As a result, other U.S. citizens or residents might be deemed to be United States shareholders of a controlled foreign corporation subject to current inclusion of Subpart F income recognized by the corporation. See Treas. Reg. section 301.7701(b)-7(a)(3).

The application of the saving clause to former citizens and former long-term residents of the United States is addressed in subparagraph (b) of paragraph 4. Under subparagraph (b), the

United States reserves for a period of ten years its right to tax former citizens and former long-term residents whose loss of citizenship or long-term resident status had as one of its principal purposes the avoidance of tax. Thus, the saving clause in subparagraph (a) applies to such persons for a period of ten years.

Subparagraph (b) is intended to allow the United States to apply section 877 of the Code. Section 877 applies to former citizens and former long-term residents of the United States whose loss of citizenship or long-term resident status had as one of its principal purposes the avoidance of tax. Under section 877, the United States generally treats an individual as having a principal purpose to avoid tax if either of the following criteria exceed established thresholds: (a) the average annual net income tax of such individual for the period of 5 taxable years ending before the date of the loss of status, or (b) the net worth of such individual as of the date of the loss of status. The thresholds are adjusted annually for inflation. Section 877(c) provides certain exceptions to these presumptions of a tax avoidance purpose.

Under section 877, the term "long-term resident" of the United States means an individual (other than a citizen of the United States) who is a lawful permanent resident of the United States in at least 8 of the 15 taxable years ending with the taxable year in which the individual ceased to be a long-term resident. Under section 877, however, an individual is not treated as a lawful permanent resident for any taxable year if such individual is treated as a resident of a foreign country for such year under the provisions of a tax treaty between the United States and the foreign country and the individual does not waive the benefits of such treaty applicable to residents of the foreign country.

Paragraph 5

Some provisions of the Convention are intended by each Contracting State to provide benefits to the citizens and residents of that Contracting State even if such benefits do not exist under internal law. Paragraph 5 sets forth certain exceptions to the saving clause that preserve these benefits for residents of the Contracting States and, in the case of the United States, citizens of the United States.

Under paragraph 5, the following provisions of the Convention are applicable to all residents of the Contracting States and, in the case of the United States, citizens of the United States, despite the general saving clause rule of subparagraph 4(a):

(1) Paragraph 2 of Article 9 (Associated Enterprises) grants the right to a correlative adjustment with respect to income tax due on profits reallocated under Article 9.

(2) Paragraph 3 of Article 9 (Associated Enterprises) generally restricts the ability of a Contracting State to change the profits of an enterprise of that Contracting State in the circumstances referred to in paragraph 1 of Article 9 if an examination of that enterprise is not initiated within seven years from the end of the taxable year with respect to which the change to the profits would take place.

(3) Paragraph 3 of Article 17 (Pensions, Social Security, Annuities, and Support Payments) provides exemptions from taxation by the Contracting State of source or the Contracting State of residence in certain circumstances for periodic payments made pursuant to a written separation agreement or a decree of divorce, separate maintenance, or compulsory support.

(4) Article 23 (Relief from Double Taxation) confirms the benefit of a credit to residents of one Contracting State and, in the case of the United States, citizens of the United States, for income taxes paid to the other Contracting State.

(5) Article 24 (Non-Discrimination) requires one Contracting State to grant national treatment to nationals of the other Contracting State in certain circumstances. Excepting this Article from the saving clause requires, for example, that the United States give such benefits to a national of Japan even if that person is a citizen of the United States.

(6) Article 25 (Mutual Agreement Procedure) may confer benefits on residents or nationals of the Contracting States. For example, the statute of limitations may be waived for refunds and the competent authorities are permitted to use a definition of a term that differs from the internal law definition. As with the foreign tax credit, these benefits are intended to be granted by a Contracting State to its residents and, in the case of the United States, its citizens.

(7) Article 28 (Diplomatic Agents and Consular Officers) confers benefits to diplomatic agents and consular officers of one Contracting State who may be residents of the other Contracting State.

Paragraph 5 also provides for a more limited exception to the saving clause in the case of benefits conferred by the United States that are intended to be granted to temporary residents of the United States (for example, holders of non-immigrant visas), but not to citizens or to persons who have acquired permanent resident in the United States. If beneficiaries of these provisions are present in the United States long enough to become residents under U.S. internal law, but do not acquire permanent resident status (*i.e.*, they do not become "green card" holders) and are not citizens of United States, the United States will continue to grant these benefits even if they conflict with statutory rules. The benefits subject to this more limited exception to the saving clause are the host country exemptions for government service salaries and pensions under Article 18 (Government Service) and certain income of visiting students, business apprentices, teachers, and researchers under Articles 19 (Students) and 20 (Teachers). The exception to the saving clause applies without limitation to the benefits conferred by Japan and thus Japan will provide the benefits of Articles 18, 19, and 20 to residents of Japan without exception.

Article 2 (Taxes Covered)

This article specifies the U.S. and Japanese taxes to which the Convention applies. Like the U.S. Model, this article does not contain a general description of the types of taxes that are covered (*i.e.*, income taxes), but only a listing of the specific taxes covered for both of the Contracting States. With several exceptions, the taxes specified in Article 2 are the only covered taxes for all purposes of the Convention. A broader coverage applies, however, for purposes of Articles 24 (Non-Discrimination) and 26 (Exchange of Information). Article 24 applies with respect to all taxes, including those imposed by state and local governments. Article 26 applies with respect to all taxes imposed at the national level. In addition, paragraph 3 of Article 8 (Shipping and Air Transport) provides for an exemption from the local inhabitant taxes and the enterprise tax in Japan in respect of the operation of ships or aircraft in international traffic by U.S. enterprises, provided that no state or local government in the United States imposes a similar tax on a in respect of such operations by Japanese enterprises. Finally, paragraph 1 of the Protocol provides for limitations on the imposition by the United States of the excise taxes imposed with respect to insurance premiums paid to foreign insurers (Code sections 4371 through 4374) and with respect to private foundations (Code sections 4940 through 4948).

Subparagraph 1(a) of the Protocol provides that the United States generally will not impose the excise tax on insurance policies issued by foreign insurers if the premiums on such policies are derived by a Japanese enterprise. The Protocol specifies that this rule applies even though the excise tax is not a covered tax under Article 2. The relief from the excise tax provided in subparagraph 1(a) of the Protocol, however, applies only to the extent that the risks covered by such premiums are not reinsured, directly or indirectly, with a person not entitled, under the Convention or any other U.S. tax treaty, to exemption from the tax. Thus, the excise tax will be imposed whenever a risk is reinsured with a person who would not be entitled to equivalent benefits, even if the reinsurance occurs in the ordinary course of business.

The rule in subparagraph 1(a) of the Protocol was considered only after a review of Japanese tax law indicated that the income tax imposed by Japan on Japanese resident insurers results in a burden that is substantial in relation to the U.S. tax on U.S. resident insurers. On the basis of this analysis, U.S. negotiators concluded that it is appropriate to waive the tax in the Convention.

Subparagraph 1(b) of the Protocol provides that the United States will not impose the excise tax with respect to private foundations on dividends or interest derived by Japanese private foundations at a rate in excess of the rates provided for in Articles 10 (Dividends) and 11 (Interest), respectively, and will not impose the excise tax with respect to private foundations on royalties or other income derived by Japanese private foundations. The effect of the rule is to make the excise tax with respect to private foundations a covered tax for purposes of the rules in Articles 10, 11, 12 (Royalties), and 21 (Other Income), which is consistent with the result in the U.S. Model.

Paragraph 1

Paragraph 1 lists the taxes in force at the time of signature of the Convention to which the Convention generally applies.

Subparagraph 1(a) provides that the Japanese taxes to which the Convention generally applies are the income tax and the corporation tax.

Subparagraph 1(b) provides that the United States taxes to which the Convention generally applies are the Federal income taxes imposed by the Code. Social security taxes (Code sections 1401, 3101, 3111 and 3301) are specifically excluded from coverage. Social security taxes are dealt with in bilateral Social Security Totalization Agreements, which are negotiated and administered by the Social Security Administration.

In the Convention, unlike the prior Convention, the accumulated earnings tax and the personal holding company tax are covered taxes because they are income taxes and they are not otherwise excluded from coverage. Under the Code, however, these taxes will not apply to most foreign corporations because of a statutory exclusion or the corporation's failure to meet a statutory requirement.

Paragraph 2

Paragraph 2 provides that the Convention will apply to any taxes that are substantially similar to those referred to in paragraph 1, and which are imposed in addition to, or in place of, the taxes referred to in paragraph 1 after November 6, 2003, the date of signature of the Convention. Paragraph 2 also provides that the U.S. and Japanese competent authorities will notify each other within a reasonable period of time of any substantial changes that have been made in their respective tax laws, or any changes in their respective non-tax laws that significantly affect their obligations under the Convention. Other laws that may affect a Contracting State's obligations under the Convention may include, for example, laws affecting bank secrecy.

Article 3 (General Definitions)

Paragraph 1

Paragraph 1 defines a number of basic terms used in the Convention. Certain other terms are defined in other articles of the Convention. For example, the term "resident of a Contracting State" is defined in Article 4 (Residence). The term "permanent establishment" is defined in Article 5 (Permanent Establishment). The term "real property" is defined in Article 8 (Real Property). The terms "dividends," "interest" and "royalties" are defined in Articles 10 (Dividends), 11 (Interest) and 12 (Royalties), respectively.

The introduction to paragraph 1 makes clear that the definitions in Article 3 apply for all purposes of the Convention, unless the context requires otherwise. This latter condition allows the Convention to be interpreted in a manner that avoids unintended results. Paragraph 2 addresses terms that are not defined in the Convention.

The term "Japan", when used in a geographical sense, is defined in subparagraph (a) to mean all the territory of Japan, including its territorial sea, in which the laws relating to Japanese tax are in force, and all the area beyond its territorial sea, including the seabed and subsoil thereof, over which Japan has jurisdiction in accordance with international law and in which the laws relating to Japanese tax are in force.

The term "United States" is defined in subparagraph (b) to mean the United States of America. When used in a geographical sense, the term "United States" includes the states, the District of Columbia and the territorial sea of the United States. The term does not include Puerto Rico, the Virgin Islands, Guam or any other U.S. possession or territory. The geographical meaning of the term "United States" also for certain purposes is extended to include the sea bed and subsoil of undersea areas adjacent to the territorial sea of the United States to the extent that the United States exercises sovereignty in accordance with international law for the purpose of natural resource exploration and exploitation of such areas. This extension of the definition applies, however, only if the person, property or activity to which the Convention is being applied is connected with such natural resource exploration or exploitation. Thus, it would not include any activity involving the sea floor of an area over which the United States exercised sovereignty for natural resource purposes if that activity was unrelated to the exploration and exploitation of natural resources.

It is understood that the term "jurisdiction" used in the definition of the term "Japan" as related to seabed and subsoil is to be interpreted in the same manner as the term "sovereignty" in the definition of the term "the United States", as described above.

Subparagraph (c) states that the terms "a Contracting State" and "the other Contracting State" mean Japan or the United States, as the context requires.

Subparagraph (d) states that the term "tax" means a Japanese tax or United States tax, as the context requires, specifically referred to in paragraph 1 of Article 2. Thus, the term "tax" generally means a tax to which the Convention applies. Several provisions, including the provisions of Articles 24 (Non-Discrimination) and Article 26 (Exchange of Information), apply to taxes other than the taxes referred to in paragraph 1 of Article 2 and therefore specifically provide that they shall apply without regard to subparagraph (d).

Subparagraph (e) defines the term "person" to include an individual, a company and any other body of persons. Paragraph 2 of the Protocol further provides that the term "any other body of persons" includes an estate, trust, and partnership. The definition of "person" is significant for a variety of reasons. For example, under Article 4, only a "person" can be a "resident" and therefore eligible for most benefits under the treaty. Also, all "persons" are eligible to claim relief under Article 25 (Mutual Agreement Procedure).

The term "company" is defined in subparagraph (f) as a body corporate or an entity treated as a body corporate for tax purposes. Although the Convention does not add "in the state in which it is organized," as does the U.S. Model, the result should be same as under the U.S. Model because the Commentary to Article 3 of the OECD Model interprets language identical to that of the Convention in a manner consistent with the U.S. Model.

Subparagraph (g) defines the term "enterprise" as applying to the carrying on of any business. Subparagraph (l) provides that the term "business" includes the performance of professional services and other activities of an independent character. Both definitions are identical to definitions recently added to the OECD Model in connection with the deletion of Article 14 (Independent Personal Services) from the OECD Model. The inclusion of the two

9

definitions in the Convention is intended to clarify that the performance of professional services or other activities of an independent character are considered to constitute an enterprise. Accordingly, income from such activities is dealt with under Article 7 (Business Profits) and not Article 21 (Other Income). The definitions are not included in the U.S. Model because the U.S. Model continues to include a separate article regarding the treatment of independent personal services.

The terms "enterprise of a Contracting State" and "enterprise of the other Contracting State" are defined in subparagraph (h) as an enterprise carried on by a resident of a Contracting State and an enterprise carried on by a resident of the other Contracting State. An enterprise of a Contracting State need not be carried on in that State. It may be carried on in the other Contracting State or a third state (*e.g.*, a U.S. corporation doing all of its business in Japan would still be a U.S. enterprise).

Subparagraph (i) defines the term "international traffic." The term means any transport by a ship or aircraft operated by an enterprise of a Contracting State, except when such transport is solely between places within the other Contracting State. This definition is applicable principally in the context of Article 8 (Shipping and Air Transport).

The exclusion from the definition of international traffic of transport solely between places within the other Contracting State means, for example, that carriage of goods or passengers solely between San Francisco and Denver by a Japanese carrier (assuming that were possible under U.S. law) would not be treated as international traffic. The substantive taxing rules of the Convention relating to the taxation of income from transport, principally Article 8 (Shipping and Air Transport), therefore, would not apply to income from such carriage. Thus, if a Japanese carrier engaged in internal U.S. traffic (assuming that were possible under U.S. law), the United States would not be required to exempt the income from that transport under Article 8. The income, however, would be treated as business profits under Article 7 (Business Profits), and therefore would be taxable in the United States only if attributable to a U.S. permanent establishment of the Japanese carrier, and then only on a net basis. The gross basis U.S. tax imposed by section 887 would never apply under the circumstances described.

If, however, goods or passengers are carried by a carrier resident in Japan from a non-U.S. port to, for example, San Francisco, and some of the goods or passengers continue on to Denver, the entire transport would be international traffic. This would be true even if the international carrier transferred the goods at the U.S. port of entry from a ship to a land vehicle, from a ship to a lighter, or even if the overland portion of the trip in the United States was handled by an independent carrier under contract with the original international carrier, so long as both parts of the trip were reflected in original bills of lading.

Finally, a "cruise to nowhere" (*i.e.*, a cruise beginning and ending in a port in the same Contracting State with no stops in a foreign port) would not constitute international traffic.

The term "national," as it relates to the United States and to Japan, is defined in clauses (i) and (ii) of subparagraph (j). This term is relevant for purposes of Article 18 (Government Services) and Article 24 (Non-Discrimination). With respect to Japan, a national is (1) any individual possessing the nationality of Japan; and (2) any juridical person deriving its status as such from the law in force in Japan. With respect to the United States, a national is (1) an individual who is a citizen of the United States, and (2) any legal person, partnership or association deriving its status as such from the law in force in the United States.

Subparagraph (k) defines the term "competent authority" for Japan and the United States respectively. The Japanese competent authority is the Minister of Finance or his authorized representative. The U.S. competent authority is the Secretary of the Treasury or his delegate. The Secretary of the Treasury has delegated the competent authority function to the Commissioner of Internal Revenue, who in turn has delegated the authority to the Director, International (LMSB). With respect to interpretative issues, the Director acts with the concurrence of the Associate Chief Counsel (International) of the Internal Revenue Service.

Subparagraph (m) defines the term "pension fund" to include any person organized under the laws of a Contracting State which is established and maintained in that Contracting State primarily to provide pension or retirement benefits or other similar remuneration, including social security payments, and which is generally exempt from income taxation with respect to such pension activities in that Contracting State. Paragraph 3 of the Protocol provides that a Japanese pension fund shall be treated as exempt from tax with respect to pension activities even though it is subject to the tax stipulated in Articles 8 or 10-2 of the Corporation Tax Law of Japan or paragraph 1 of Article 20 of its supplementary provisions. This tax is not an income tax, but rather a tax intended to prevent the excess funding of pension funds. The base of this tax is the amount contributed to a pension fund less amounts withdrawn, without regard to the income earned on pension assets. This tax has no effect on the amount received by beneficiaries.

In the case of the United States, the term "pension fund" includes the following plans under existing U.S. law: qualified plans under section 401(a), individual retirement plans (including individual retirement plans that are part of a simplified employee pension plan that satisfies section 408(k), individual retirement accounts, individual retirement annuities, section 408(p) accounts, and Roth IRAs under section 408A), section 457 governmental plans, section 403(a) qualified annuity plans, section 403(b) plans, and any fund identical or substantially similar to the foregoing schemes that are established pursuant to legislation introduced after the date of signature of the Convention. Section 401(k) plans qualify as pension funds because a 401(k) plan is a type of 401(a) plan.

Paragraph 2

Paragraph 2 provides that in the application of the Convention, any term used but not defined in the Convention will have the meaning that it has under the law of the Contracting State whose tax is being applied, unless the context requires otherwise. The paragraph makes clear that if the term is defined under both the tax and non-tax laws of a Contracting State, the definition in the tax law will take precedence over the definition in the non-tax laws. Finally, there also may be cases where the tax laws of a Contracting State contain multiple definitions of the same term. In such a case, the definition used for purposes of the particular provision at issue, if any, should be used.

If the meaning of a term cannot be readily determined under the law of a Contracting State, or if there is a conflict in meaning under the laws of the two Contracting States that creates difficulties in the application of the Convention, the competent authorities may agree to the meaning of a term for purposes of applying the Convention pursuant to the provisions of Article 25 (Mutual Agreement Procedure). This agreed meaning need not conform to the meaning of the term under the laws of either Contracting State.

The reference in paragraph 2 to the internal law of a Contracting State means the law in effect at the time the treaty is being applied, not the law as in effect at the time the treaty was signed. The use of "ambulatory" definitions, however, may lead to results that are at variance with the intentions of the negotiators and of the Contracting States when the treaty was negotiated and ratified. The reference in both paragraphs 1 and 2 to the "context otherwise requir[ing]" a definition different from the treaty definition, in paragraph 1, or from the internal law definition of the Contracting State whose tax is being imposed, under paragraph 2, refers to a circumstance where the result intended by the Contracting States is different from the result that would obtain under either the paragraph 1 definition or the statutory definition. This allows the Convention to be interpreted in a manner that avoids unintended results.

Article 4 (Residence)

This Article sets forth rules for determining whether a person is a resident of a Contracting State for purposes of the Convention. As a general matter only residents of the Contracting States may claim the benefits of the Convention. The determination of residence under Article 4 is to be used only for purposes of the Convention. The fact that a person is determined to be a resident of a Contracting State under Article 4 does not necessarily entitle that person to the benefits of the Convention. In addition to being a resident, a person also must qualify for benefits under the limitations on benefits provisions of Article 22 (Limitation on Benefits) in order to receive benefits conferred on residents of a Contracting State.

The determination of residence for treaty purposes looks first to a person's liability to tax as a resident under the respective taxation laws of the Contracting States. As a general matter, a person who, under those laws, is a resident of one Contracting State and not of the other need look no further. For purposes of the Convention, that person is a resident of the Contracting State in which he is resident under internal law. If, however, a person is a resident of both Contracting States under their respective taxation laws, paragraphs 2 through 4 provide tie-breaker rules to assign a single Contracting State of residence to such a person, where possible, for purposes of the Convention.

Paragraph 5 provides specific rules applicable to individuals who are resident but not domiciled in Japan and therefore are subject to a remittance system of taxation. Paragraph 6 provides specific rules applicable to income earned through fiscally transparent entities.

Paragraph 1

The term "resident of a Contracting State" is defined in paragraph 1. In general, this definition incorporates the definitions of residence in U.S. and Japanese law by referring to a resident as a person who, under the laws of a Contracting State, is subject to tax there by reason of his domicile, residence, citizenship, place of head or main office, place of incorporation or any other similar criterion. Thus, residents of the United States include aliens who are considered U.S. residents under Code section 7701(b). Place of management is not included as a criterion because neither U.S. law nor Japanese law look to place of management as a relevant criterion for determining residence.

Certain entities that are nominally subject to tax but that in practice are rarely required to pay tax also would generally be treated as residents and therefore accorded treaty benefits. For example, RICs, REITs and REMICs are all residents of the United States for purposes of the Convention. Although the income earned by these entities normally is not subject to U.S. tax in the hands of the entity, such entities are taxable to the extent that they do not currently distribute their profits, and therefore may be regarded as "liable to tax." They also must satisfy a number of requirements under the Code in order to be entitled to the special tax treatment.

Paragraph 1 also provides that the term "resident of a Contracting State" includes that Contracting State and any political subdivision or local authority thereof, and certain tax-exempt entities such as pension funds and charitable or similar organizations regardless of whether they are generally liable for income tax in the Contracting State where they are established. This provision is intended to clarify the generally accepted practice of treating an entity such as a pension fund or a charitable organization that would be liable for tax as a resident under the internal law of a Contracting State but for a specific exemption from tax (either complete or partial) as a resident of that Contracting State. Pension funds are defined in subparagraph 1(m) of Article 3 (General Definitions).

Charitable or similar entities that are considered residents of a Contracting State consist of any person organized under the laws of that Contracting State and established or maintained in that Contracting State exclusively for a religious, charitable, educational, scientific, artistic, cultural, or public purposes, even if the person is exempt from tax in that Contracting State. Thus, a section 501(c) organization (such as a U.S. charity) that is generally exempt from tax under U.S. law is a resident of the United States for purposes of the Convention.

A person who is liable to tax in a Contracting State only in respect of income from sources within that State or capital situated therein or of profits attributable to a permanent establishment in that State will not be treated as a resident of that Contracting State for purposes of the Convention. Thus, a consular official of Japan who is posted in the United States, who may be subject to U.S. tax on U.S. source investment income but is not taxable in the United States on non-U.S. source income, would not be considered a resident of the United States for purposes of the Convention. (See Code section 7701(b)(5)(B)). Similarly, an enterprise of Japan with a permanent establishment in the United States is not, by virtue of that permanent establishment, a resident of the United States. The enterprise generally is subject to U.S. tax only with respect to its income that is attributable to the U.S. permanent establishment, and generally is not subject to U.S. tax with respect to its worldwide income, as it would be if it were a U.S. resident.

Paragraph 2

Paragraph 2 contains an exception to the general rule of paragraph 1 that residence under internal law also determines residence under the Convention. The exception applies with respect to a U.S. citizen or alien lawfully admitted for permanent residence (*i.e.*, a "green card" holder). Under paragraph 1, a person is considered a resident of a Contracting State for purposes of the Convention if he is liable to tax in that Contracting State by reason of citizenship. Although this rule applies to both Contracting States, only the United States taxes its non-resident citizens in the same manner as its residents. In addition, aliens admitted to the United States for permanent residence qualify as U.S. residents under the first sentence of paragraph 1 because they are taxed by the United States as residents, regardless of where they physically reside.

Under the exception of paragraph 2, a U.S. citizen or green card holder who is not also a resident of Japan will be treated as a resident of the United States for purposes of the Convention, and, thereby entitled to treaty benefits, only if he meets two conditions. First, he must have a substantial presence (see section 7701(b)(3)), permanent home or habitual abode in the United States. This rule requires that the U.S. citizen or green card holder have a reasonably strong economic nexus with the United States. Second, he must not be treated as a resident of a state other than Japan under any treaty between Japan and a third state. This rule prevents a U.S. citizen or green card holder who is a resident of a country other than the United States or Japan from choosing the benefits of the Convention over those provided by the treaty between Japan and his country of residence. If the U.S. citizen or green card holder's country of residence does not have a treaty with Japan, however, then he will be treated as a resident of the United States as long as he meets the first requirement of an economic nexus. If such a person is a resident of both the United States and Japan, whether or not he is to be treated as a resident of the United States for purposes of the Convention is determined by the tie-breaker rules of paragraph 3.

Thus, for example, an individual resident of Mexico who is a U.S. citizen by birth, but who, has never lived in the United States, would not be entitled to benefits under the Convention. However, a U.S. citizen who is transferred to Mexico for two years would be entitled to benefits under the Convention if he maintains a permanent home or habitual abode in the United States and is not a resident of Mexico for purposes of the Japan-Mexico tax treaty. If he were treated as a resident of Mexico under the Japan-Mexico tax treaty, he could claim only the benefits of that treaty, even if the Convention would provide greater benefits.

The fact that a U.S. citizen who does not have close ties to the United States may not be treated as a U.S. resident under the Convention does not alter the application of the saving clause of paragraph 4 of Article 1 (General Scope) to that citizen. For example, a U.S. citizen who pursuant to the "citizen/green card holder" rule is not considered to be a resident of the United States still is taxable on his worldwide income under the generally applicable rules of the Code.

Paragraph 3

If, under the laws of the two Contracting States and thus under paragraph 1, an individual is deemed to be a resident of both Contracting States, a series of tie-breaker rules are provided in paragraph 3 to determine a single Contracting State of residence for that individual for purposes of the Convention. These tests are to be applied in the order in which they are stated.

The first test is based on where the individual has a permanent home. If that test is inconclusive because the individual has a permanent home available to him in both Contracting States, he will be deemed to be a resident of the Contracting State where his personal and economic relations are closest (*i.e.*, the location of his "centre of vital interests"). If that test is also inconclusive, or if he does not have a permanent home available to him in either Contracting State, he will be deemed to be a resident of the Contracting State where he has an habitual abode. If he has an habitual abode in both Contracting States or in neither of them, he will be deemed to be a resident of the Contracting State of which he is a national. If he is a national of both Contracting States or of neither, the single Contracting State of residence of the individual will be settled by the competent authorities. An individual who is deemed to be a resident of a Contracting State by reason of the tests in paragraph 3 will be deemed to be a resident only of that Contracting State for purposes of the Convention.

Paragraph 4

Dual residents other than individuals (*e.g.*, companies, trusts, and estates) are addressed by paragraph 4. If such a person is, under the rules of paragraph 1, a resident of both Contracting States, the competent authorities shall seek to determine a single Contracting State of residence for that person for purposes of the Convention.

If the competent authorities do not reach an agreement on the single Contracting State of residence of a dual resident other than an individual, that person shall not be considered a resident of either Contracting State for the purposes of claiming any benefits provided by the Convention. That person may, however, be entitled to benefits of the Convention that are not limited to residents, such as the benefits of Articles 24 (Non-Discrimination) and 25 (Mutual Agreement Procedure). Thus, for example, a Contracting State cannot discriminate against a dual resident company, and such a company can bring issues to the competent authorities. In addition, information relating to dual resident companies can be exchanged under the Convention because, by its terms, Article 26 (Exchange of Information) is not limited to residents of the Contracting States.

Dual residents that are not individuals also may be treated as a resident for purposes other than that of obtaining benefits under the Convention. For example, if a dual resident company pays a dividend to a resident of Japan, the U.S. paying agent would withhold on that dividend at the appropriate treaty rate because reduced withholding is a benefit enjoyed by the resident of Japan, not by the dual resident. The dual resident company that paid the dividend would, for this purpose, be treated as a resident of the United States under the Convention.

Paragraph5

Paragraph 5 is included in the Convention because Japan continues to maintain a remittance system of taxation for individuals who are resident but not domiciled in Japan. Such persons are subject to tax in Japan on non-Japanese source income only to the extent the income or gains are remitted to Japan. Under paragraph 5, such persons are entitled to the benefits of the Convention in order to reduce or eliminate tax only to the extent that the relevant income is remitted to or received in Japan. For example, if a Japanese resident who is not domiciled in Japan maintains a brokerage account in Singapore into which is paid $100 in U.S.-source dividend income, the United States may impose withholding tax at the statutory rate of 30 percent because the dividend income will not be taxed in Japan as it has not been remitted to Japan. If the dividend income instead is paid into a brokerage account in Tokyo, the Japanese resident will be subject to tax in Japan and the United States will reduce the rate of withholding tax to 10 percent.

Paragraph 6

Paragraph 6 provides specific rules for the treatment of income derived though fiscally transparent entities such as partnerships and certain estates and trusts. In general, fiscally transparent entities are entities the income of which is taxed at the beneficiary, member, or participant level. Entities that are subject to tax, but with respect to which tax may be relieved under an integrated system, are not considered fiscally transparent entities. Entities falling under this description in the United States include partnerships, common investment trusts under section 584, and business entities such as limited liability companies ("LLCs") that are treated as partnerships for U.S. tax purposes.

Under subparagraphs (a) and (c), an item of income derived from one Contracting State through an entity that organized in the other Contracting State or a third state and that is treated as a fiscally transparent entity under the tax laws of the other Contracting State generally will be eligible for the benefits of the Convention to the extent such benefits would be granted if the income were directly derived by the beneficiaries, members or participants. Under subparagraphs (b), (d), and (e), an item of income derived from one Contracting State through an entity that is organized in the other Contracting State or a third state and that is not treated as a fiscally transparent entity under the tax laws of the other Contracting State generally will be eligible for the benefits of the Convention only if the entity is a resident of that other Contracting State. These results are consistent with provisions addressing fiscally transparent entities in recent U.S. treaties and with U.S. domestic law pursuant to regulations under section 894(c).

Subparagraph (a) provides that an item of income that is derived from a Contracting State through an entity organized in the other Contracting State and that is treated as the income of the beneficiaries, members or participants of that entity under the tax laws of that other Contracting State shall be eligible for the benefits of the Convention that would be granted if it were directly derived by a beneficiary, member or participant of that entity who is a resident of that other Contracting State, to the extent such beneficiaries, members or participants are residents of that other Contracting State and satisfy any other conditions specified in the Convention. Such item of income shall be eligible for the benefits of the Convention without regard to whether the income is treated as the income of the beneficiaries, members, or participants under the laws of the first-mentioned Contracting State.

For example, if a Japanese company pays interest to a U.S. LLC that is treated as a partnership for U.S. tax purposes, the interest income will be eligible for the benefits of the

Convention to the extent it is treated under the taxation laws of the United States as the income of one or more U.S. residents that satisfy any other conditions specified for eligibility for the benefits of the Convention. In the case of a U.S. LLC that is treated as a partnership for U.S. tax purposes, the tax laws of the United States normally would treat the interest income derived through the U.S. LLC as the income of its partners or members. Thus, if all of the partners or members of the U.S. LLC were U.S. residents that satisfy any other conditions for eligibility for the benefits of the Convention, then all of the interest income would be eligible for the benefits of the Convention. If U.S. residents owned a share of the U.S. LLC, then the interest income attributable to the U.S. residents would be eligible for the benefits of the Convention.

The interest income will be eligible for the benefits of the Convention that would be granted if it were received directly by the partner or member; thus, if the partners or members of the U.S. LLC are all banks that are U.S. residents and satisfy all other conditions specified in the Convention, the interest income would be exempt from source-basis taxation in Japan under paragraph 3 of Article 11.

Interest income derived through the U.S. LLC will not be eligible for the benefits of the Convention to the extent it is treated under the tax laws of the United States as the income of a person that is not a U.S. resident or that does not satisfy any other conditions specified in the Convention, such as the conditions in the limitations on benefits provisions of Article 22. (If, however, the country in which such person is treated as resident for tax purposes, as determined under the laws of that country, has an income tax treaty with Japan, such person may be entitled to claim a benefit under that treaty.)

The same result obtains even if the U.S. LLC were viewed differently under the tax laws of Japan (*e.g.*, as not fiscally transparent in the example above where the entity is treated as a partnership for U.S. tax purposes). Thus, the same result obtains without regard to whether the income is treated as the income of the partners or members of the U.S. LLC under the tax laws of Japan.

The rules of paragraph 6, including subparagraph (a), may be applicable to trusts as well. For example, if X, a resident of the United States, creates a revocable trust in the United States and names persons resident in a third country as the beneficiaries of the trust, income derived through the trust would be treated as the income of X under the tax laws of the United States. If interest income arising in Japan is derived through the trust, the interest income will be eligible for the benefits of the Convention to the extent it is treated under the taxation laws of the United States as the income of one or more U.S. residents that satisfy any other conditions specified for eligibility for the benefits of the Convention. Thus, in this case, because the interest income is treated as the income of X under the tax laws of the United States, the interest income will be eligible for the benefits of the Convention to the extent that X satisfies any other conditions for eligibility for such benefits. The same result obtains even if the U.S. trust were viewed as a taxable entity under the tax laws of Japan.

Subparagraph (b) provides that an item of income that is derived from a Contracting State through an entity organized in the other Contracting State and that is treated as the income of the entity under the tax laws of that other Contracting State shall be eligible for the benefits of the

Convention if such entity is a resident of that other Contracting State and satisfies any other conditions for the benefits specified in the Convention. Such item of income shall be eligible for the benefits of the Convention without regard to whether the income is treated as the income of the entity under the laws of the first-mentioned Contracting State.

For example, if a Japanese company pays interest to a U.S. contractual joint venture that elects to be treated as a corporation for U.S. tax purposes, the interest income will be eligible for the benefits of the Convention if the joint venture is a U.S. resident and it satisfies any other conditions for the benefits specified in the Convention. That result obtains even if the U.S. contractual joint venture were viewed differently under the tax laws of Japan (*e.g.*, not as an entity but rather as an aggregate of its owners). Thus, that result obtains without regard to whether the income is treated as the income of the U.S. contractual joint venture under the tax laws of Japan.

Similarly, if a U.S. company pays interest to a Japanese Yugen-Kaisha, which is treated as a taxable entity for Japanese tax purposes, the interest income will be eligible for the benefits of the Convention if the Yugen-Kaisha is a Japanese resident and it satisfies any other conditions for the benefits specified in the Convention. That result obtains even if the Japanese Yugen-Kaisha were viewed differently under the tax laws of the United States (*e.g.*, as a partnership pursuant to an election under the U.S. entity classification rules). Thus, that result obtains without regard to whether the income is treated as the income of the Japanese Yugen-Kaisha under the tax laws of the United States.

Subparagraph (c) provides the same result as subparagraph (a) in the case of an entity organized in a state other the Contracting States. Thus, an item of income that is derived from a Contracting State through an entity organized in a third state and that is treated as the income of the beneficiaries, members or participants of that entity under the tax laws of the other Contracting State shall be eligible for the benefits of the Convention that would be granted if it were directly derived by a beneficiary, member or participant of that entity that is a resident of that other Contracting State, to the extent such beneficiaries, members or participants are residents of that other Contracting State and satisfy any other conditions specified in the Convention. Such item of income shall be eligible for the benefits of the Convention without regard to whether the income is treated as the income of the beneficiaries, members, or participants under the laws of the first-mentioned Contracting State or the state in which the entity is organized.

For example, if a Japanese company pays interest to an Australian proprietary company that is treated as a partnership for U.S. tax purposes, the interest income will be eligible for the benefits of the Convention to the extent it is treated under the taxation laws of the United States as the income of one or more U.S. residents that satisfy any other conditions specified for eligibility for the benefits of the Convention. In the case of an Australian proprietary company that is treated as a partnership for U.S. tax purposes, the tax laws of the United States normally would treat the interest income derived through the Australian proprietary company as the income of its partners or members. Thus, if all of the partners or members of the Australian proprietary company were U.S. residents that satisfy any other conditions for eligibility to the benefits of the Convention, then all of the interest income would be eligible for the benefits of the Convention. If U.S. residents owned a share of the Australian proprietary company, then the interest income attributable to the U.S. residents would be eligible for the benefits of the Convention.

The same result obtains even if the Australian proprietary company were viewed differently under the tax laws of Japan (*e.g.*, as not fiscally transparent in the example above where the entity is treated as a partnership for U.S. tax purposes). Thus, the same result obtains without regard to whether the income is treated as the income of the partners or members of the Australian proprietary company under the tax laws of Japan. Similarly, the characterization of the entity in the country of organization is also irrelevant. Thus, the same result obtains in the example above without regard to whether the income is treated as the income of the partners or members of the Australian proprietary company under the tax laws of Australia.

Subparagraphs (d) and (e) provide that an item of income that is derived from a Contracting State through an entity not organized in the other Contracting State and that is treated as the income of the entity under the tax laws of that other Contracting State shall not be eligible for the benefits of the Convention. Such item of income shall not be eligible for the benefits of the Convention regardless of whether the income is treated as the income of the beneficiaries, members or participants of the entity under the laws of the Contracting State of source or the state in which the entity is organized.

Subparagraph (d) provides this rule in the case of an entity organized in a state other than the Contracting States. Thus, an item of income that is derived from a Contracting State through an entity organized in a third state and that is treated as the income of the entity under the tax laws of the other Contracting State shall not be eligible for the benefits of the Convention. For example, if a U.S. company pays interest to an Australian proprietary company that is treated as a corporation for Japanese tax purposes, the interest income will not be eligible for the benefits of the Convention. That result obtains even if the Australian proprietary company were viewed differently under the tax laws of the United States (*e.g.*, if it elects to be treated as a partnership for U.S. tax purposes). Thus, the same result obtains without regard to whether the income is treated as the income of the partners or members of the Australian proprietary company under the tax laws of United States. Similarly, the characterization of the entity in the country of organization is also irrelevant. Thus, the same result obtains in the example above without regard to whether the income is treated as the income of the Australian proprietary company under the tax laws of Australia.

Subparagraph (e) provides the same result as subparagraph (d) in the context of an entity organized in the Contracting State from which the item of income is derived. Thus, an item of income that is derived from a Contracting State through an entity organized in that Contracting State and that is treated as the income of the entity under the tax laws of the other Contracting State shall not be eligible for the benefits of the Convention. For example, if a U.S. company pays interest to a U.S. LLC that is treated as a corporation for Japanese tax purposes, the interest income will not be eligible for the benefits of the Convention. That result obtains even if the U.S. LLC were viewed differently under the tax laws of the United States (*e.g.*, if it is treated as a partnership for U.S. tax purposes). Thus, the same result obtains without regard to whether the income is treated as the income of the partners or members of the U.S. LLC under the tax laws of United States.

One case that is not dealt with specifically by paragraph 6 is the case of an item of income that is derived from a Contracting State through an entity organized in that Contracting State and that is treated as the item of income of the beneficiaries, members or participants of that entity under the tax laws of the other Contracting State. As discussed below, the result in this case depends on whether the entity is liable to tax in the Contracting State in which it is organized.

If an item of income that is derived from a Contracting State through an entity organized in that Contracting State is treated as the item of income of the entity under the tax laws of that Contracting State, then that Contracting State is not prevented from taxing the entity in accordance with its domestic law under the saving clause of paragraph 4 of Article 1. Paragraph 6 of Article 4 is not an exception to the saving clause. Accordingly, a Contracting State may tax an entity that is treated as a resident of that Contracting State under its tax law. For example, if a U.S. LLC with Japanese members elects to be taxed as a corporation for U.S. tax purposes, the United States may tax that U.S. LLC on its worldwide income on a net basis, without regard to whether Japan views the LLC as fiscally transparent. Thus, if a U.S. company pays interest to a U.S. LLC that elects to be treated as a corporation for U.S. tax purposes, the interest income will not be eligible for the benefits of the Convention. In the case of income derived in the United States, this result is consistent with the result in Treas. Reg. § 1.894-1(d)(2)(ii) (providing rules for the eligibility for treaty benefits of items of income paid by U.S. entities that are not fiscally transparent under U.S. law but are fiscally transparent under the laws of the jurisdiction of the person claiming treaty benefits).

If, however, the entity is not liable to tax under the tax laws of the Contracting State in which it is organized, then income derived through the entity is treated as the income of the beneficiaries, members or participants of that entity under the tax laws of both Contracting States. In such a case, the saving clause generally is not relevant to the taxation of income derived through the entity by the Contracting State in which it is organized. Under the principles underlying subparagraphs (a) and (c), such income will be eligible for the benefits of the Convention to the extent that the beneficiaries, members or participants are residents of the other Contracting State and satisfy any other conditions specified in the Convention. For example, if a U.S. corporation pays interest income to a U.S. partnership that is not liable to tax as an entity under the tax laws of either the United States or Japan and the income is treated as the income of the partners of the U.S. partnership under the tax laws of both the United States and Japan, then the income will be entitled to the benefits of the Convention to the extent the partners of the U.S. partnership are Japanese residents that satisfy any other condition specified in the Convention. This fact pattern is unlikely to arise in practice because, under the domestic law of Japan, an entity generally either is treated as taxable or is ignored. Because this fact pattern is unlikely to arise in practice, and because in cases where it does arise there is no potential conflict between the domestic laws of both Contracting States, no specific rule is provided to address this fact pattern.

Paragraph 13 of the Protocol provides specific rules regarding the application of the Convention to an arrangement created by a sleeping partnership (Tokumei Kumiai) contract or similar contract. In general, these rules allow the United States and Japan to apply their respective domestic tax laws to income derived subject to such an arrangement and to distributions made pursuant to the arrangement.

The Japanese tax law treats income derived subject to such an arrangement as the income of the active partner or operator. The operator then is entitled to a deduction for amounts paid to the sleeping partner or investor, who takes such amounts into income as a distribution from the arrangement.

Subparagraph 13(a) of the Protocol provides that the United States may treat such an arrangement as not a resident of Japan, and may treat income derived subject to the arrangement as not derived by any participant in the arrangement. Thus, the United States will not grant the benefits of the Convention to any income derived subject to the arrangement. For example, if a U.S. corporation pays interest income to an arrangement created by a sleeping partnership (Tokumei Kumiai) contract, then the United States will not grant the benefits of the Convention to that interest income even if the operator and investor in the arrangement are Japanese residents.

Subparagraph 13(b) of the Protocol provides that Japan may impose tax at source, in accordance with its domestic law, on distributions that a person makes pursuant to a sleeping partnership (Tokumei Kumiai) contract and that are deductible in computing the taxable income in Japan of that person. For example, if a Japanese person acting as the operator in the arrangement makes a distribution pursuant to the arrangement to another person that is deductible in computing the taxable income in Japan of the Japanese person, then Japan may impose tax at source on the distribution even if the investor is a U.S. resident.

Article 5 (Permanent Establishment)

This Article defines the term "permanent establishment," a term that is significant for several articles of the Convention. The existence of a permanent establishment in a Contracting State is necessary under Article 7 (Business Profits) for the taxation by that Contracting State of business profits of a resident of the other Contracting State. Articles 10, 11 and 12 (dealing with dividends, interest, and royalties, respectively) provide for reduced rates of tax at source on payments of these items of income to a resident of the other Contracting State only when such items are not attributable to a permanent establishment that the recipient has in the source State. The concept is also relevant in determining which Contracting State may tax certain gains under Article 13 (Gains) and certain "other income" under Article 21 (Other Income).

The Article follows closely both the U.S. Model and the OECD Model provisions.

Paragraph 1

The basic definition of the term "permanent establishment" is contained in paragraph 1. As used in the Convention, the term means a fixed place of business through which the business of an enterprise is wholly or partly carried on. As indicated in the OECD Commentary to Article 5 (see paragraphs 4 through 8), a general principle to be observed in determining whether a permanent establishment exists is that the place of business must be "fixed" in the sense that a particular building or physical location is used by the enterprise for the conduct of its business, and it must be foreseeable that the enterprise's use of this building or other physical location will be more than temporary.

Paragraph 2

Paragraph 2 lists a number of types of fixed places of business that constitute a permanent establishment. This list is illustrative and non-exclusive. Paragraph 2 provides that the term permanent establishment includes a place of management, a branch, an office, a factory, a workshop, and a mine, oil or gas well, quarry or other place of extraction of natural resources.

Paragraph 3

This paragraph provides rules to determine whether a building site or a construction, assembly or installation project, or an installation or drilling rig or ship used for the exploration of natural resources, constitutes a permanent establishment for the contractor, driller, etc. An activity does not create a permanent establishment unless the site, project, etc. lasts or continues for a period of more than twelve months. Paragraph 3 refers to "exploration" and not "exploitation" in this context because exploitation activities are defined to constitute a permanent establishment under subparagraph (f) of paragraph 2. Thus, a drilling rig does not constitute a permanent establishment if a well is drilled in only six months, but if production begins in the following month the well becomes a permanent establishment as of the date on which production begins.

The twelve-month test applies separately to each site or project. The twelve-month period begins when work (including preparatory work carried on by the enterprise) physically begins in a Contracting State. A series of contracts or projects by a contractor that are interdependent both commercially and geographically are to be treated as a single project for purposes of applying the twelve-month threshold test. For example, the construction of a housing development would be considered as a single project even if each house were constructed for a different purchaser. Several drilling rigs operated by a drilling contractor in the same sector of the continental shelf also normally would be treated as a single project.

In applying this paragraph, time spent by a sub-contractor on a building site is counted as time spent by the general contractor at the site for purposes of determining whether the general contractor has a permanent establishment. However, for the sub-contractor itself to be treated as having a permanent establishment, the sub-contractor's activities at the site must last for more than 12 months. If a sub-contractor is on a site intermittently, then for purposes of applying the 12-month rule time is measured from the first day the sub-contractor is on the site until the last day (i.e., intervening days that the sub-contractor is not on the site are counted).

These interpretations of the Article are based on the Commentary to paragraph 3 of Article 5 of the OECD Model, which contains language substantially the same as that in the

Convention (except for the absence in the OECD Model of a rule for drilling rigs). These interpretations are consistent with the generally accepted international interpretation of the relevant language in paragraph 3 of Article 5 of the Convention.

If the twelve-month threshold is exceeded, the site or project constitutes a permanent establishment from the first day of activity.

Paragraph 4

This paragraph contains exceptions to the general rule of paragraph 1, listing specific activities that may be carried on through a fixed place of business, but which nevertheless do not create a permanent establishment. The use of facilities solely to store, display or deliver merchandise belonging to an enterprise does not constitute a permanent establishment of that enterprise. The maintenance of a stock of goods belonging to an enterprise solely for the purpose of storage, display or delivery, or solely for the purpose of processing by another enterprise does not give rise to a permanent establishment of the first-mentioned enterprise. The maintenance of a fixed place of business solely for the purpose of purchasing goods or merchandise, or for collecting information, for the enterprise, or for other activities that have a preparatory or auxiliary character for the enterprise, such as advertising or the supply of information, do not constitute a permanent establishment of the enterprise. Thus, as explained in paragraph 22 of the OECD Commentary, a news bureau of a newspaper would not constitute a permanent establishment of the newspaper.

Subparagraph 4(f) provides that a combination of the activities described in the other subparagraphs of paragraph 4 will not give rise to a permanent establishment if the combination results in an overall activity that is of a preparatory or auxiliary character. This combination rule, derived from the OECD Model, differs from that in the U.S. Model. In the U.S. Model, any combination of otherwise excepted activities is deemed not to give rise to a permanent establishment, without the additional requirement that the combination, as distinct from each constituent activity, be preparatory or auxiliary. If preparatory or auxiliary activities are combined, the combination generally also will be of a character that is preparatory or auxiliary. If, however, this is not the case, a permanent establishment may result from a combination of such activities.

Paragraph 5

Paragraphs 5 and 6 specify when activities carried on by an agent on behalf of an enterprise create a permanent establishment of that enterprise. Under paragraph 5, a dependent agent of an enterprise is deemed to be a permanent establishment of the enterprise if the agent has and habitually exercises an authority to conclude contracts in the name of the enterprise. If, however, the agent's activities are limited to those activities specified in paragraph 4 which would not constitute a permanent establishment if carried on by the enterprise through a fixed place of business, the agent is not a permanent establishment of the enterprise.

The Convention uses the term "in the name of that enterprise" as in the OECD Model, rather than "binding on the enterprise" as in the U.S. Model. There is no substantive difference.

As indicated in paragraph 32 to the OECD Commentary on Article 5, paragraph 5 of the Article is intended to encompass a person who "concludes contracts which are binding on the enterprise, even if those contracts are not actually in the name of the enterprise."

The contracts referred to in paragraph 5 are those relating to the essential business operations of the enterprise rather than ancillary activities. For example, if the agent has no authority to conclude contracts in the name of the enterprise with its customers for the sale of the goods produced by the enterprise, but it can enter into service contracts in the name of the enterprise for the enterprise's business equipment used in the agent's office, this contracting authority would not fall within the scope of the paragraph, even if exercised regularly.

Paragraph 6

Under paragraph 6, an enterprise is not deemed to have a permanent establishment in a Contracting State merely because it carries on business in that State through an independent agent, including a broker or general commission agent, if the agent is acting in the ordinary course of his business as an independent agent. Thus, there are two conditions that must be satisfied: the agent must be both legally and economically independent of the enterprise, and the agent must be acting in the ordinary course of its business in carrying out activities on behalf of the enterprise.

Whether the agent and the enterprise are independent is a factual determination. Among the questions to be considered are the extent to which the agent operates on the basis of instructions from the enterprise. An agent that is subject to detailed instructions regarding the conduct of its operations or comprehensive control by the enterprise is not legally independent.

In determining whether the agent is economically independent, a relevant factor is the extent to which the agent bears business risk. Business risk refers primarily to risk of loss. An independent agent typically bears risk of loss from its own activities. In the absence of other factors that would establish dependence, an agent that shares business risk with the enterprise, or has its own business risk, is economically independent because its business activities are not integrated with those of the principal. Conversely, an agent that bears little or no risk from the activities it performs is not economically independent and therefore is not described in paragraph 6.

Another relevant factor in determining whether an agent is economically independent is whether the agent has an exclusive or nearly exclusive relationship with the principal. Such a relationship may indicate that the principal has economic control over the agent. A number of principals acting in concert also may have economic control over an agent. The limited scope of the agent's activities and the agent's dependence on a single source of income may indicate that the agent lacks economic independence. It should be borne in mind, however, that exclusivity is not in itself a conclusive test; an agent may be economically independent notwithstanding an exclusive relationship with the principal if it has the capacity to diversify and acquire other clients without substantial modifications to its current business and without substantial harm to its business profits. Thus, exclusivity should be viewed merely as a pointer to further investigation of the relationship between the principal and the agent. Each case must be addressed on the basis of its own facts and circumstances.

Paragraph 7

This paragraph clarifies that a company that is a resident of a Contracting State is not deemed to have a permanent establishment in the other Contracting State merely because it controls, or is controlled by, a company that is a resident of that other Contracting State or that carries on business in that other Contracting State. The determination whether a permanent establishment exists is made solely on the basis of the factors described in paragraphs 1 through 6 of the Article. Whether a company is a permanent establishment of a related company, therefore, is based solely on those factors and not on the ownership or control relationship between the companies.

Article 6 (Income from Real Property)

Paragraph 1

The first paragraph of Article 6 states the general rule that income of a resident of a Contracting State derived from real property situated in the other Contracting State may be taxed in the Contracting State in which the property is situated. The paragraph specifies that income from real property includes income from agriculture and forestry. Income from agriculture and forestry thus are dealt with in Article 6 rather than in Article 7 (Business Profits). Paragraph 3 clarifies that the income referred to in paragraph 1 also includes income from any use of real property, including, but not limited to, income from direct use by the owner (in which case income may be imputed to the owner for tax purposes) and rental income from the letting of real property.

This Article does not grant an exclusive taxing right to the situs State; the situs State is merely given the primary right to tax. The Article does not impose any limitation in terms of rate or form of tax on the situs State. Thus, the Convention does not include paragraph 5 of Article 6 of the U.S. Model, regarding the allowance of an election to be taxed on a net basis on income from real property. Net basis taxation, however, is available under the domestic tax laws of the United States and Japan. Thus, taxpayers generally should be able to obtain the same tax treatment in the Contracting State where the real property is situated regardless of whether the income is treated as business profits attributable to a permanent establishment or income from real property.

Paragraph 2

The term "real property" is defined in paragraph 2 generally by reference to the internal law definition in the situs State. In the case of the United States, the term "real property" has the meaning given to it by Treas. Reg. section 1.897-1(b). Consistent with Treas. Reg. § 1.897-1(b), paragraph 2 provides that the term "real property" shall include: property accessory to real property; livestock and equipment used in agriculture and forestry; rights to which the provisions of general law respecting real property apply; usufruct of real property; and rights to variable or fixed payments as consideration for the working of, or the right to work, mineral deposits and other natural resources. Paragraph 2 also provides that ships and aircraft are not regarded as real property.

The term "real property" is defined in paragraph 2 for all purposes of the Convention. In addition to its use in Article 6, the term is used in Articles 10 (Dividends) and 13 (Gains).

Paragraph 3

Paragraph 2 makes clear that all forms of income derived from the exploitation of real property are taxable in the Contracting State in which the property is situated. In the case of a net lease of real property, the gross rental payment (before deductible expenses incurred by the lessee) may be treated as income from the property. Income from the disposition of an interest in real property, however, is not considered "derived" from real property and is not dealt with in this article. The taxation of that income is addressed in Article 13 (Gains). Also, the interest paid on a mortgage on real property and distributions by a U.S. Real Estate Investment Trust are not dealt with in Article 6. Such payments would fall under Article 10 (Dividends), 11 (Interest) or 13 (Gains). Finally, dividends paid by a United States Real Property Holding Corporation are not considered to be income from the exploitation of real property; such payments would fall under Article 10 (Dividends) or 13 (Gains).

Paragraph 4

This paragraph specifies that the basic rule of paragraph 1, as elaborated in paragraph 3, applies to income from real property of an enterprise. This clarifies that the situs country may tax the real property income (including rental income) of a resident of the other Contracting State in the absence of attribution to a permanent establishment in the situs State. This provision represents an exception to the general rule under Article 7 (Business Profits) that income must be attributable to a permanent establishment in order to be taxable in the host state.

Article 7 (Business Profits)

This Article provides rules for the taxation by a Contracting State of the profits of an enterprise of the other Contracting State. Subparagraph (g) of Article 3 (General Definitions) defines the term "enterprise" as applying to the carrying on of any business.

Paragraph 1

Paragraph 1 states the general rule that profits of an enterprise of one Contracting State may not be taxed by the other Contracting State unless the enterprise carries on business in that other Contracting State through a permanent establishment (as defined in Article 5 (Permanent Establishment)) situated there. When that condition is met, the Contracting State in which the permanent establishment is situated may tax the enterprise on the income that is attributable to the permanent establishment.

Although the Convention does not include a definition of "profits," the term is intended generally to have the same meaning as the term "business profits" under paragraph 7 of Article 7 of the U.S. Model. The term also covers income from independent personal services because the Convention does not contain a separate article dealing with independent personal services, as discussed in connection with the definitions of "enterprise" and "business" in the Technical Explanation to Article 3 (General Definitions) above. Thus, the term "profits" generally means income derived from any trade or business.

In accordance with this broad definition, the term "profits" includes income attributable to notional principal contracts and other financial instruments to the extent that the income is attributable to a trade or business of dealing in such instruments or is otherwise related to a trade or business (as in the case of a notional principal contract entered into for the purpose of hedging currency risk arising from an active trade or business). Any other income derived from such instruments is, unless specifically covered in another article, dealt with under Article 21 (Other Income).

The term also includes income earned by an enterprise from the furnishing of personal services. Thus, a consulting firm resident in one Contracting State whose employees or partners perform services in the other Contracting State through a permanent establishment may be taxed in that other Contracting State on a net basis under Article 7, and not under Article 14 (Income from Employment), which applies only to income of employees. This change is consistent with the OECD Model, pursuant to which income derived from professional services or other activities of an independent character is dealt with under Article 7 as business profits. With respect to the enterprise's employees themselves, however, their salary remains subject to Article 14.

Because this article applies to income earned by an enterprise from the furnishing of personal services, the article also applies to income derived by a partner resident in a Contracting State that is attributable to personal services performed in the other Contracting State through a partnership with a permanent establishment in that other Contracting State. Income which may be taxed under this article includes all income attributable to the permanent establishment in respect of the performance of the personal services carried on by the partnership (whether by the partner himself, other partners in the partnership, or by employees assisting the partners) and any income from activities ancillary to the performance of those services (*e.g.*, charges for facsimile services). Income that is not derived from the performance of personal services and that is not ancillary thereto (*e.g.*, rental income from subletting office space) is governed by other articles of the Convention.

The application of Article 7 to a service partnership may be illustrated by the following example: a legal partnership has five partners (who agree to split profits equally), four of whom are resident and perform personal services only in Japan at Office A, and one of whom performs personal services at Office B, a permanent establishment in the United States. In this case, the four partners of the partnership resident in Japan may be taxed in the United States in respect of their share of the income attributable to the permanent establishment, Office B. The services giving rise to income which may be attributed to the permanent establishment would include not only the services performed by the one resident partner, but also, for example, if one of the four other partners came to the United States and worked on an Office B matter there, the income in respect of those services. Income from the services performed by the visiting partner would be subject to tax in the United States regardless of whether the visiting partner actually visited or used Office B while performing services in the United States.

Paragraph 4 of the Protocol incorporates into the Convention the rule of Code section 864(c)(6). Like the Code section on which it is based, paragraph 7 provides that any profits attributable to a permanent establishment during its existence is taxable in accordance with the principles of Article 7 in the Contracting State where the permanent establishment is situated, even if the receipt of profits is deferred until after the permanent establishment ceases to exist. This rule applies with respect to profits under Article 7, as well as dividends under paragraph 7 of Article 10 (Dividends), interest under paragraph 6 of Article 11 (Interest), royalties under paragraph 3 of Article 12 (Royalties), and other income under paragraph 2 of Article 21 (Other Income). A similar result is provided by paragraph 4 of Article 13 (Gains) with respect to gains from the alienation of any property, other than real property, forming part of the business property of a permanent establishment.

The effect of this rule can be illustrated by the following example. Assume a company that is a resident of Japan and that maintains a permanent establishment in the United States winds up the permanent establishment's business at the end of year 1 but has deferred the receipt of profits attributable to the permanent establishment until year 2. Despite the fact that Article 7's threshold requirement for U.S. taxation is not met in year 2 because the company has no permanent establishment in the United States in that year, the United States may tax the deferred income payment recognized by the company in year 2.

Paragraph 2

Paragraph 2 provides rules for the attribution of business profits to a permanent establishment. The Contracting States will attribute to a permanent establishment the profits that it would have earned had it been a distinct and separate enterprise engaged in the same or similar activities under the same or similar conditions and dealing wholly independently with the enterprise of which it is a permanent establishment. The "attributable to" concept of paragraph 2 is analogous but not entirely equivalent to the "effectively connected" concept in Code section 864(c). The profits attributable to a permanent establishment may be from sources within or without a Contracting State.

The language of paragraph 2, when combined with paragraph 3 dealing with the allowance of deductions for expenses incurred for the purposes of earning the profits, incorporates the arm's-length standard for purposes of determining the profits attributable to a permanent establishment. As noted below with respect to Article 9 (Associated Enterprises), the United States generally interprets the arm's length standard in a manner consistent with the OECD Transfer Pricing Guidelines.

Paragraph 2 of the Notes confirms that the principles as set out in paragraph 1 of Article 9 (Associated Enterprises) may apply in determining the profits attributable to a permanent establishment. In applying these principles, it is necessary to take into account the different economics that arise from operating through a single legal entity rather than through separate legal entities. For example, an entity that operates through branches rather than separate subsidiaries will have lower capital requirements because all of the assets of the entity are available to support all of the entity's liabilities (with some exceptions attributable to local regulatory restrictions). This is the reason that most commercial banks and some insurance companies operate through branches rather than subsidiaries. The benefit that comes from such lower capital costs must be allocated among the branches in an appropriate manner. This issue does not arise in the case of an enterprise that operates through separate entities, since each entity will have to be separately capitalized or will have to compensate another entity for providing capital (usually through a guarantee).

Under U.S. domestic regulations, internal "transactions" generally are not recognized because they do not have legal significance. In contrast, under the provision of paragraph 2 of the Notes, such internal dealings may be used to allocate income in cases where the dealings accurately reflect the allocation of risk within the enterprise. One example is that of global trading in securities. In many cases, banks use internal swap transactions to transfer risk from one branch to a central location where traders have the expertise to manage that particular type of risk. Under the Convention, such a bank may also use such swap transactions as a means of allocating income between the branches, if use of that method is the "best method" within the meaning of regulation section 1.482-1(c). The books of a branch will not be respected, however, when the results are inconsistent with a functional analysis. So, for example, income from a transaction that is booked in a particular branch (or home office) will not be treated as attributable to that location if the sales and risk management functions that generate the income are performed in another location.

It is also permissible to use methods other than separate accounting to determine the arm's length profits of a permanent establishment when such a method would be permissible under the principles of paragraph 1 of Article 9. This might occur, for example, when the affairs of the permanent establishment are so closely bound up with those of the head office that it would be impossible to disentangle them on any strict basis of accounts. Because the use of profits methods is permissible under the principles of paragraph 1 of Article 9 and therefore paragraph 2, it is not necessary for the Convention to include a provision corresponding to paragraph 4 of Article 7 of the OECD Model.

Unlike the U.S. Model, paragraph 2 does not explicitly provide that the profits attributed to a permanent establishment include only those profits derived from that permanent establishment's assets or activities. This rule nevertheless is understood to apply since, even though the OECD Model also does not expressly provide such a limitation, it generally is understood to be implicit in paragraph 1 of Article 7 of the OECD Model. Further, this rule is consistent with the application of the arm's-length standard for purposes of determining the profits attributable to a permanent establishment. Thus, the "residual force of attraction" rule of section 864(c)(3) is not applicable to determining the profits attributable to a permanent establishment.

Paragraph 3

This paragraph is the same as paragraph 3 of Article 7 of the OECD Model. Paragraph 3 provides that in determining the profits of a permanent establishment, deductions shall be allowed for the expenses incurred for the purposes of the permanent establishment, ensuring that business profits will be taxed on a net basis. This rule is not limited to expenses incurred exclusively for the purposes of the permanent establishment, but includes expenses incurred for the purposes of the enterprise as a whole, or that part of the enterprise that includes the permanent establishment. Deductions are to be allowed regardless of which accounting unit of the enterprise books the expenses, so long as they are incurred for the purposes of the permanent establishment. For example, a portion of the interest expense recorded on the books of the home office in one Contracting State may be deducted by a permanent establishment in the other if properly allocable thereto. The amount of expense that must be allowed as a deduction is determined by applying the arm's length principle.

As noted above, paragraph 2 of the Notes provides that the principles of paragraph 1 of Article 9 (Associated Enterprises) may apply in determining the profits attributable to a permanent establishment. Accordingly, a permanent establishment may deduct payments made to its head office or another branch in compensation for services performed for the benefit of the branch. The method to be used in calculating that amount will depend on the terms of the arrangements between the branches and head office. For example, the enterprise could have a policy, expressed in writing, under which each business unit could use the services of lawyers employed by the head office. At the end of each year, the costs of employing the lawyers would be allocated to each business unit according to the amount of services used by that business unit during the year. Since this appears to be a kind of cost-sharing arrangement and the allocation of costs is based on the benefits received by each business unit, it would be an acceptable means of determining a permanent establishment's deduction for legal expenses. Alternatively, the head office could agree to employ lawyers at its own risk, and to charge an arm's length price for legal services performed for a particular business unit. If the lawyers were under-utilized, and the "fees" received from the business units were less than the cost of employing the lawyers, then the head office would bear the excess cost. If the "fees" exceeded the cost of employing the lawyers, then the head office would keep the excess to compensate it for assuming the risk of employing the lawyers. If the enterprise acted in accordance with this agreement, this method would be an acceptable alternative method for calculating a permanent establishment's deduction for legal expenses.

Paragraph 2 of the Notes also specifies that a permanent establishment cannot be funded entirely with debt, but must have sufficient capital to carry on its activities as if it were a distinct and separate enterprise. To the extent that the permanent establishment does not have such capital, a Contracting State may attribute such capital to the permanent establishment and deny an interest deduction to the extent necessary to reflect that capital attribution. The method prescribed by U.S. domestic law for making this attribution is found in Treas. Reg. Section 1.882-5. Section 1.882-5(a)(2) states that the method is to be used in determining the amount of interest expense attributable to the business profits of a permanent establishment under U.S. tax treaties. Accordingly, a Japanese taxpayer may continue to use that method for determining its interest expense if it so chooses.

However, section 1.882-5 does not take into account the fact that some assets are more risky than other assets. An independent enterprise would need less capital to support a perfectly-hedged U.S. Treasury security than it would need to support an equity security or other asset with significant market and/or credit risk. Accordingly, in some cases section 1.882-5 would require a taxpayer to allocate more capital to the United States (and therefore would reduce the taxpayer's interest deduction) than is appropriate. To address these cases, paragraph 2 of the Notes allows a taxpayer to apply a more flexible approach that takes into account the relative risk of its assets in the various jurisdictions in which it does business. In particular, in the case of financial institutions other than insurance companies, the amount of capital attributable to a permanent establishment is determined by allocating the institution's total equity between its various offices on the basis of the proportion of the financial institution's risk-weighted assets attributable to each of them. This recognizes the fact that financial institutions are in many cases required to risk-weight their assets for regulatory purposes and, in other cases, will do so for business reasons even if not required to do so by regulators. However, the taxpayer is not required to apply this treaty method for determining its interest deduction. As noted above, it may choose to apply the rule of Treas. Reg. Section 1.882-5 instead if that produces less U.S. taxable income in the taxpayer's particular circumstances.

Paragraph 4

Paragraph 4 provides that nothing in this Article shall affect the application of any law of a Contracting State relating to the determination of the tax liability of any person in cases where the information available to the competent authority of that State is inadequate to determine the profits to be attributed to a permanent establishment. The Internal Revenue Service would have this power even in the absence of such a specific provision. In any such case, however, determination of the profits of the permanent establishment must be consistent with the principles stated in this Article (i.e., the Contracting State must seek to reflect arm's length pricing and appropriate deductions of expenses).

Paragraph 5

Paragraph 5 provides that no profits can be attributed to a permanent establishment merely because it purchases goods or merchandise for the enterprise of which it is a part. This paragraph is essentially identical to paragraph 4 of Article 7 of the U.S. Model. This rule applies only to an office that performs functions for the enterprise in addition to purchasing. The income attribution issue does not arise if the sole activity of the permanent establishment is the purchase of goods or merchandise because such activity does not give rise to a permanent establishment under Article 5. A common situation in which paragraph 5 is relevant is one in which a permanent establishment purchases raw materials for the enterprise's manufacturing operation conducted outside the United States and sells the manufactured product. While business profits may be attributable to the permanent establishment with respect to its sales activities, no profits are attributable to it with respect to its purchasing activities.

Paragraph 6

Paragraph 6 provides that profits shall be determined by the same method each year, unless there is good reason to change the method used. This rule assures consistent tax treatment over time for permanent establishments. It limits the ability of both the Contracting State and the enterprise to change accounting methods to be applied to the permanent establishment. It does not, however, restrict a Contracting State from imposing additional requirements, such as the rules under Code section 481, to prevent amounts from being duplicated or omitted following a change in accounting method.

Paragraph 7

Paragraph 7 coordinates the provisions of Article 7 and other provisions of the Convention. Under this paragraph, when business profits include items of income that are dealt with separately under other articles of the Convention, the provisions of those articles will, except when they specifically provide to the contrary, take precedence over the provisions of Article 7. For example, the taxation of dividends will be determined by the rules of Article 10 (Dividends), and not by Article 7, except where, as provided in paragraph 7 of Article 10, the dividend is attributable to a permanent establishment. In the latter case the provisions of Article 7 apply. Thus, an enterprise of one Contracting State deriving dividends from the other State may not rely on Article 7 to exempt those dividends from tax at source if they are not attributable to a permanent establishment of the enterprise in the other Contracting State. By the same token, if the dividends are attributable to a permanent establishment in the other Contracting State, the dividends may be taxed on a net income basis at the source Contracting State full corporate tax rate, rather than on a gross basis under Article 10 (Dividends).

As provided in Article 8 (Shipping and Air Transport), income derived from shipping and air transport activities in international traffic described in that Article is taxable only in the country of residence of the enterprise regardless of whether it is attributable to a permanent establishment situated in the source Contracting State.

Relation to Other Articles

This Article is subject to the saving clause of subparagraph 4(a) of Article 1 (General Scope) of the Convention. Thus, if a citizen of the United States who is a resident of Japan under the treaty derives profits from the United States that are not attributable to a permanent establishment in the United States, the United States may, subject to the special foreign tax credit rules of paragraph 3 of Article 23 (Relief from Double Taxation), tax those profits as part of the worldwide income of the citizen, notwithstanding the provision of paragraph 1 of this Article which would exempt the income from U.S. tax.

The benefits of this Article are also subject to Article 22 (Limitation on Benefits). Thus, an enterprise of Japan that derives income effectively connected with a U.S. trade or business may not claim the benefits of Article 7 unless the resident carrying on the enterprise qualifies for such benefits under Article 22.

Article 8 (Shipping and Air Transport)

This Article governs the taxation of profits from the operation of ships and aircraft in international traffic, and from the use of containers. The term "international traffic" is defined in subparagraph 1(i) of Article 3 (General Definitions). The taxation of gains from the alienation of ships, aircraft or containers is dealt with not in this Article but in paragraphs 5 and 6 of Article 13 (Gains).

Paragraph 1

Paragraph 1 provides that profits from the operation in international traffic of ships or aircraft carried on by an enterprise of a Contracting State are taxable only in that Contracting State. Because paragraph 7 of Article 7 (Business Profits) defers to Article 8 with respect to shipping income, such income derived by a resident of one of the Contracting States may not be taxed in the other Contracting State even if the enterprise has a permanent establishment in that other Contracting State. Thus, if a U.S. airline has a ticket office in Japan, Japan may not tax the airline's profits attributable to that office under Article 7. Since entities engaged in international transportation activities normally will have many permanent establishments in a number of countries, the rule avoids difficulties that would be encountered in attributing income to multiple permanent establishments if the income were covered by Article 7 (Business Profits).

Paragraph 2

The income from the operation of ships or aircraft in international traffic that is exempt from tax under paragraph 1 is defined in paragraph 2. In addition to income derived directly from the operation of ships and aircraft in international traffic, this definition also includes certain items of rental income that are closely related to those activities. First, income of an enterprise of a Contracting State from the rental of ships or aircraft on a full basis (*i.e.*, with crew) when such ships or aircraft are used in international traffic is income of the lessor from the operation of ships and aircraft in international traffic and, therefore, is exempt from tax in the other Contracting State under paragraph 1. Also, paragraph 2 encompasses income from the lease of ships or aircraft on a bareboat basis (*i.e.*, without crew) when the income is incidental to other income of the lessor from the operation of ships or aircraft in international traffic. Thus, the coverage of Article 8 of the Convention is generally consistent with Article 8 of the OECD Model although narrower than the U.S. Model, which also covers rentals from bareboat leasing that are not incidental to the operation of ships or aircraft by the lessee. The classes of income derived by an enterprise of a Contracting State from the rental of ships and aircraft not included in this Article are covered by Article 7 (Business Profits) and thus are subject to tax in the other Contracting State only to the extent not attributable to a permanent establishment in that other Contracting State.

Paragraph 2 also clarifies, consistent with the Commentary to Article 8 of the OECD Model, that income earned by an enterprise from the inland transport of property or passengers within either Contracting State falls within Article 8 if the transport is undertaken as part of the international transport of property or passengers by the enterprise. Thus, if a U.S. shipping company contracts to carry property from Japan to a U.S. city and, as part of that contract, it transports the property by truck from its point of origin to an airport in Japan (or it contracts with a trucking company to carry the property to the airport) the income earned by the U.S. shipping company from the overland leg of the journey would be taxable only in the United States. Similarly, Article 8 would apply to income from lighterage undertaken as part of the international transport of goods.

Finally, certain non-transport activities that are an integral part of the services performed by a transport company are understood to be covered in paragraph 1, though they are not specified in paragraph 2. These include, for example, the performance of some maintenance or catering services by one airline for another airline, if these services are incidental to the provision of those services by the airline for itself. Income earned by concessionaires, however, is not covered by Article 8. See paragraphs 7 through 10.1 of the Commentary to Article 8 of the OECD Model.

Paragraph 3

Paragraph 3 provides for an exemption from certain local taxes in Japan in respect of the operation of ships or aircraft in international traffic by U.S. enterprises, provided that no state or local government in the United States imposes a similar tax on a Japanese enterprise in respect of such operations. In particular, paragraph 3 provides that a U.S. enterprise will be exempt from the local inhabitant taxes and the enterprise tax in Japan in respect of the operation of ships or aircraft in international traffic provided that no state or local government in the United States imposes a similar tax on a Japanese enterprise in respect of such operations. Absent paragraph 3, Japan could apply these taxes to U.S. shipping and aircraft enterprises because the local inhabitant tax and the enterprise tax are not covered taxes under Article 2. Paragraph 3 generally is consistent with the current treatment of local Japanese taxes by the prior Convention and the notes thereto.

Paragraph 1 of the Notes further provides that if a state or local authority of the United States seeks to levy a tax similar to these taxes on the profits of any Japanese enterprise from the operation of ships or aircraft in international taxes in circumstances where the Convention would preclude the imposition of Federal income tax on those profits, the Government of the United States will use its best endeavors to persuade that political subdivision or local authority to refrain from imposing such tax. At the present time, it is the understanding of the Treasury Department that no such state or local tax is imposed on Japanese airlines and shipping companies in the United States.

Paragraph 4

Under this paragraph, profits of an enterprise of a Contracting State from the use, maintenance or rental of containers (including equipment for their transport) are exempt from tax in the other Contracting State except where such containers are used solely within the other Contracting State. This result is the same as that under paragraph 3 of Article 8 of the U.S. Model, which provides that profits of an enterprise from the use, maintenance or rental of containers (including equipment for their transport) "that are used for the transport of goods in international traffic" are exempt from tax in the other Contracting State. Because the definition of "international traffic" in subparagraph 1(i) of Article 3 (General Definitions) is limited to transport by a ship or aircraft operated by an enterprise of a Contracting State, however, a reference to "international traffic" in paragraph 4 would have reached results inconsistent with the U.S. Model, for example, in a case of a U.S. enterprise that rented containers for use in the international transport by a ship operated by an enterprise of a third State.

Paragraph 4 exempts profits of an enterprise of a Contracting State from containers from tax in the other Contracting State regardless of whether the recipient of the income is engaged in the operation of ships or aircraft in international traffic, and regardless of whether the enterprise has a permanent establishment in that other Contracting State. By contrast, Article 8 of the OECD Model covers only income from the use, maintenance or rental of containers that is incidental to other income from international traffic.

Paragraph 5

This paragraph clarifies that the provisions of Article 8 also apply to profits derived by an enterprise of a Contracting State from participation in a pool, joint business or international operating agency. This refers to various arrangements for international cooperation by carriers in shipping and air transport. For example, airlines from two countries may agree to share the transport of passengers between the two countries. They each will fly the same number of flights per week and share the revenues from that route equally, regardless of the number of passengers that each airline actually transports. Paragraph 5 makes clear that with respect to each carrier the Article exempts all the income earned by that carrier with respect to the pool, and not just the income derived directly by that carrier. This paragraph corresponds to paragraph 4 of Article 8 of the U.S. Model.

Relation to Other Articles

This Article is subject to the saving clause of subparagraph 4(a) of Article 1 (General Scope) of the Convention. Thus, if a citizen of the United States who is a resident of Japan derives profits from the operation of ships or aircraft in international traffic, notwithstanding the exclusive residence country taxation in paragraph 1 of Article 8, the United States may, subject to the special foreign tax credit rules of paragraph 3 of Article 23 (Relief from Double Taxation), tax those profits as part of the worldwide income of the citizen. (This is an unlikely situation, however, because non-tax considerations (*e.g.*, insurance) generally result in shipping activities being carried on in corporate form.)

As with other benefits of the Convention, the benefit of exclusive residence country taxation under Article 8 is available to an enterprise only if it is entitled to benefits under Article 22 (Limitation on Benefits).

Article 9 (Associated Enterprises)

This Article incorporates in the Convention the arm's-length principle reflected in the OECD Transfer Pricing Guidelines and U.S. domestic transfer pricing provisions, particularly Code section 482 and the regulations thereunder. It provides that when related enterprises engage in a transaction on terms that are not arm's-length, the Contracting States may make appropriate adjustments to the taxable income and tax liability of such related enterprises to reflect what the income and tax of these enterprises with respect to the transaction would have been had there been an arm's-length relationship between them.

Paragraph 1

This paragraph addresses the situation where an enterprise of a Contracting State is related to an enterprise of the other Contracting State, and there are arrangements or conditions imposed between the enterprises in their commercial or financial dealings that are different from those that would have existed in the absence of the relationship. Under these circumstances, the Contracting States may adjust the income (or loss) of the enterprise to reflect what it would have been in the absence of such a relationship and thus in accordance with the arm's length principle.

The paragraph identifies the relationships between enterprises that serve as a prerequisite to application of the Article. As the Commentary to Article 9 of the OECD Model makes clear, the necessary element in these relationships is effective control, which is also the standard for purposes of section 482. Thus, the Article applies if an enterprise of one Contracting State participates directly or indirectly in the management, control, or capital of the enterprise of the other Contracting State. Also, the Article applies if the same third person or persons participate directly or indirectly in the management, control, or capital of enterprises of different Contracting States. For this purpose, all types of control are included (*i.e.*, whether or not legally enforceable and however exercised or exercisable).

Paragraph 5 of the Protocol clarifies the basis for determining the profits of an enterprise under the arm's-length principle. The arm's-length analysis is generally based on a comparison of the conditions in the transactions made between associated enterprises and those made between independent enterprises. The qualifier "generally" is used because in some cases an analysis based on transactions between independent enterprises is not possible, either because comparable transactions have not taken place or because data regarding such transactions is not available to the associated enterprises. Paragraph 5 sets out five factors that could affect comparability: (1) the comparability of the property or services transferred; (2) the functions of the associated enterprises, taking into account the assets used and risks assumed by the associated enterprises; (3) the contractual terms between the associated enterprises; (4) the economic circumstances of the associated enterprises, and (5) the business strategies pursued by the associated enterprises. These five comparability factors correspond to those set out in the OECD Transfer Pricing Guidelines (paragraphs 1.19 through 1.35), and are consistent with U.S. domestic transfer-pricing provisions, particularly Treas. Reg. section 1.482-1(d).

Paragraph 3 of the Notes sets out the understanding of the Contracting States that double taxation can be avoided only through a common understanding of the principles to be applied in resolving transfer pricing case. Paragraph 3 of the Notes further provides that the Contracting States shall undertake to conduct transfer pricing examinations of enterprises and evaluate applications for advance pricing arrangements in accordance with the OECD Transfer Pricing Guidelines. The domestic transfer pricing rules, including the transfer pricing methods, of each

Contracting State may be applied in resolving transfer pricing cases under the Convention only to the extent that they are consistent with the OECD Transfer Pricing Guidelines.

The OECD Transfer Pricing Guidelines reflect the consensus of OECD member countries (including the United States and Japan) on the application of the arm's length principle in the context of Article 9 of the OECD Model and of their respective bilateral treaties that are consistent with the OECD Model. Thus, it is generally understood that transfer pricing cases in the context of mutual agreement procedures between OECD member countries should be resolved with reference to the OECD Transfer Pricing Guidelines. Paragraph 3 of the Notes confirms and extends this understanding. Paragraph 3 reflects the intention of each Contracting State to conduct transfer pricing examinations of enterprises related to enterprises of the other Contracting State in accordance with the OECD Transfer Pricing Guidelines, rather than to utilize the OECD Transfer Pricing Guidelines solely in the context of the mutual agreement procedures under Article 25 of the Convention. Further, paragraph 3 clarifies that while each country may apply its domestic transfer rules in resolving transfer pricing cases, such rules may be applied only to the extent that they are consistent with the OECD Transfer Pricing Guidelines. The U.S. transfer pricing provisions, particularly Code section 482 and the regulations thereunder, generally are consistent with the current OECD Transfer Pricing Guidelines.

The reference in paragraph 3 of the Notes to the OECD Transfer Pricing Guidelines is to that document as it continues to evolve, rather than to the document as it exists at a certain point in time. It is well understood that the OECD Transfer Pricing Guidelines are periodically updated to reflect the ongoing development of international standards in this area. Thus, as the OECD Transfer Pricing Guidelines change, there may be corresponding changes in the respective obligations of the Contracting States under the Convention. Because the OECD is a consensus organization, the OECD Transfer Pricing Guidelines cannot be updated without the acquiescence of all of its members, including the United States and Japan.

The fact that a transaction is entered into between such related enterprises does not, in and of itself, mean that a Contracting State may adjust the income (or loss) of one or both of the enterprises under the provisions of this Article. If the conditions of the transaction are consistent with those that would be made between independent persons, the income arising from that transaction should not be subject to adjustment under this Article.

Similarly, the fact that associated enterprises may have concluded arrangements, such as cost sharing arrangements or general services agreements, is not in itself an indication that the two enterprises have entered into a non-arm's-length transaction that should give rise to an adjustment under paragraph 1. Both related and unrelated parties enter into such arrangements (*e.g.*, joint venturers may share some development costs). As with any other kind of transaction, when related parties enter into an arrangement, the specific arrangement must be examined to see whether or not it meets the arm's-length standard. In the event that it does not, an appropriate adjustment may be made, which may include modifying the terms of the agreement or recharacterizing the transaction to reflect its substance.

The "commensurate with income" standard for determining appropriate transfer prices for intangibles, added to Code section 482 by the Tax Reform Act of 1986, was designed to operate consistently with the arm's-length standard. The implementation of this standard in the section 482 regulations is in accordance with the general principles of paragraph 1 of Article 9 of the Convention, as interpreted by the OECD Transfer Pricing Guidelines. See paragraphs 6.28 through 6.35 of the Transfer Pricing Guidelines.

It is understood that the Contracting States preserve their rights to apply internal law provisions relating to adjustments between related parties. They also reserve the right to make adjustments in cases involving tax evasion or fraud. Such adjustments -- the distribution, apportionment, or allocation of income, deductions, credits or allowances -- are permitted even if they are different from, or go beyond, those authorized by paragraph 1 of the Article, as long as they accord with the general principles of paragraph 1 (*i.e.*, that the adjustment reflects what would have transpired had the related parties been acting at arm's length). For example, while paragraph 1 explicitly allows adjustments of deductions in computing taxable income, it does not deal with adjustments to tax credits. It does not, however, preclude such adjustments if they can be made under internal law. The OECD Model reaches the same result. See paragraph 4 of the Commentary to Article 9.

This Article also permits tax authorities to deal with thin capitalization issues. They may, in the context of Article 9, scrutinize more than the rate of interest charged on a loan between related persons. They also may examine the capital structure of an enterprise, whether a payment in respect of that loan should be treated as interest, and, if it is treated as interest, under what circumstances interest deductions should be allowed to the payer. Paragraph 2 of the Commentary to Article 9 of the OECD Model, together with the U.S. observation set forth in paragraph 15 thereof, sets forth a similar understanding of the scope of Article 9 of the OECD Model in the context of thin capitalization.

Paragraph 2

When a Contracting State has made an adjustment that is consistent with the provisions of paragraph 1, and the other Contracting State agrees that the adjustment was appropriate to reflect arm's-length conditions, that other Contracting State is obligated to make a correlative adjustment (sometimes referred to as a "corresponding adjustment") to the tax liability of the related person in that other Contracting State. Unlike the Convention the OECD Model does not specify that the other Contracting State must agree with the initial adjustment before it is obligated to make the correlative adjustment, but the Commentary makes clear that the paragraph is to be read that way.

When an adjustment under Article 9 has been made, one of the parties will have in its possession funds that it would not have had at arm's length. The question arises as to how to treat these amounts in excess of the arm's length amounts. As explained in the Commentary to Article 9 of the OECD Model, Article 9 leaves the treatment of so-called "secondary adjustments" to the laws of the Contracting States.

In the United States the general practice is to treat such funds as a dividend or contribution to capital, depending on the relationship between the parties. Under certain circumstances, the parties may be permitted to restore the funds to the party that would have the funds at arm's length, and to establish an account payable pending restoration of the funds. See Rev. Proc. 99-32, 1999-2 C.B. 296.

Articles 11 (Interest), 12 (Royalties), and 21 (Other Income) provide specific rules in the context of adjustments in the amount of interest, royalties, or other income. These rules are discussed below in the explanation of paragraph 8 of Article 11, paragraph 4 of Article 12, and paragraph 3 of Article 21.

The competent authorities are authorized by paragraph 3 of Article 25 (Mutual Agreement Procedure) to consult, if necessary, to resolve any differences in the application of the provisions of paragraphs 1 or 2 of Article 9. For example, there may be a disagreement over whether an adjustment made by a Contracting State under paragraph 1 was appropriate.

If a correlative adjustment is made under paragraph 2, it is to be implemented, pursuant to paragraph 2 of Article 25 (Mutual Agreement Procedure), notwithstanding any time limits or other procedural limitations in the law of the Contracting State making the adjustment. If a taxpayer has entered a closing agreement (or other written settlement) with the United States prior to bringing a case to the competent authorities, the U.S. competent authority will endeavor only to obtain a correlative adjustment from Japan. See Rev. Proc. 2002-52, 2002-31 I.R.B. 242, Section 7.04.

Paragraph 3

Paragraph 3 provides a procedural limitation on the authority of a Contracting State under paragraph 1 to adjust the amount of profits of an enterprise with respect to arrangements between that enterprise and a related person in the other Contracting State, when such arrangements differ from those that would obtain between unrelated persons. Paragraph 3 provides that a Contracting State may not make an adjustment with respect to the profits of an enterprise in the circumstances referred to in paragraph 1 if an examination of the enterprise is not initiated within seven years from the end of the taxable year in which the profits that would be subject to change would have accrued to that enterprise.

The limitation in paragraph 3 is unlikely to apply in the case of the United States because of the generally applicable three-year statute of limitations under Code section 6501 and the policy of the Internal Revenue Service to initiate and close examinations on as current a basis as possible even where extensions to the statute of limitations could be obtained. Further, the limitation in paragraph 3 generally could not apply in the case of Japan under current Japanese tax law because of the generally applicable six-year statute of limitations that generally is not subject to extension.

The provisions of paragraph 3 shall not apply in the case of fraud or willful default or if the inability to initiate an examination within the seven-year period is attributable to the actions or inaction of that enterprise. A significant purpose of this limitation on the general rule of paragraph 3 is to prevent taxpayers from using the general rule to attempt to avoid adjustments by delaying the conduct of examinations in prior periods.

Relationship to Other Articles

The saving clause of subparagraph 4(a) of Article 1 (General Scope) does not apply to paragraphs 2 and 3 of Article 9 by virtue of the exceptions to the saving clause in paragraph 5 of Article 1. Thus, even if the statute of limitations has run, a refund of tax can be made by a Contracting State to its residents in order to implement a correlative adjustment under paragraph 2. Statutory or procedural limitations, however, cannot be overridden to impose additional tax, because paragraph 2 of Article 1 provides that the Convention cannot restrict any statutory benefit. Similarly, the procedural limitation of paragraph 3 may apply to a potential adjustment by a Contracting State to the profits of an enterprise of that Contracting State that also is a resident of that Contracting State.

Article 10 (Dividends)

Article 10 provides rules for the taxation of dividends paid by a company that is a resident of one Contracting State to a beneficial owner that is a resident of the other Contracting State. The article provides for full residence country taxation of such dividends and a limited source-country right to tax. Article 10 also provides rules for the imposition of a tax on branch profits by the Contracting State of source. Finally, the article prohibits a Contracting State from imposing taxes on undistributed earnings of a company resident in the other Contracting State, other than a branch profits tax.

Paragraph 1

The right of a shareholder's country of residence to tax dividends arising in the source country is preserved by paragraph 1, which permits a Contracting State to tax its residents on dividends paid to them by a company that is a resident of the other Contracting State. For dividends from any other source paid to a resident, Article 21 (Other Income) grants the residence country exclusive taxing jurisdiction (other than for dividends attributable to a permanent establishment in the other Contracting State).

Paragraph 2

The Contracting State of source also may tax dividends, subject to the limitations of paragraphs 2 and 3 if the beneficial owner of the dividends is a resident of the other Contracting State. Paragraph 2 generally limits the maximum rate of withholding tax in the Contracting State of source on dividends paid by a company resident in that Contracting State to 10 percent of the gross amount of the dividend. If, however, the beneficial owner of the dividend is a company that is a resident of the other Contracting State and that owns shares representing at least 10 percent of the voting power of the company paying the dividend, then under subparagraph 2(a) the maximum rate of withholding tax in the Contracting State of source is limited to 5 percent of the gross amount of the dividend. Indirect ownership of voting shares (through tiers of corporations) is taken into account for the purpose of determining eligibility for the 5 percent maximum rate of withholding tax. Shares are considered voting shares if they provide the power to elect, appoint or replace any person vested with the powers ordinarily exercised by the board of directors of a U.S. corporation.

The benefits of paragraph 2 may be granted at the time of payment by means of reduced rate of withholding tax at source. It also is consistent with the paragraph for tax to be withheld at the time of payment at full statutory rates, for example in cases where it is not possible to determine eligibility for the lower rate of withholding tax, and the treaty benefit to be granted by means of a subsequent refund, so long as such procedures are applied in a reasonable manner.

Paragraph 2, and also paragraph 3 described below, do not affect the taxation of the profits out of which the dividends are paid. The taxation by a Contracting State of the income of its resident companies is governed by the internal law of the Contracting State, subject to the provisions of paragraph 4 of Article 24 (Non-Discrimination).

The term "beneficial owner" is not defined in the Convention, and is, therefore, defined as under the internal law of the Contracting State imposing tax (*i.e.*, the source country). The beneficial owner of the dividend for purposes of Article 10 is the person to which the dividend income is attributable for tax purposes under the laws of the source State. Thus, if a dividend paid by a corporation that is a resident of one of the Contracting States (as determined under Article 4 (Residence)) is received by a nominee or agent that is a resident of the other Contracting State on behalf of a person that is not a resident of that other Contracting State, the dividend is not entitled to the benefits of this Article. However, a dividend received by a nominee on behalf of a resident of that other Contracting State would be entitled to benefits. These limitations are confirmed by paragraph 12 of the OECD Commentary to Article 10. See also paragraph 24 of the Commentary to Article 1 of the OECD Model.

Companies holding shares through fiscally transparent entities such as partnerships may be considered for purposes of this paragraph to hold their proportionate interest in the shares held by the intermediate entity under the rules of paragraph 6 of Article 4 (Residence). As a result, companies holding shares through such entities may be able to claim the benefits of subparagraph 2(a) of Article 10 under certain circumstances. The 5 percent maximum rate of withholding tax applies when the company's proportionate share of the shares held by the intermediate entity meets the 10 percent threshold. Whether this ownership threshold is satisfied often will require an analysis of the partnership or trust agreement.

The determination of whether the ownership threshold of subparagraph 2(a) is met for purposes of the 5 percent maximum rate of withholding tax is made on the date on which entitlement to the dividends is determined. Thus, in the case of a dividend from a U.S. company, the determination of whether the ownership threshold is met generally would be made on the dividend record date. In the case of a dividend from a Japanese company, paragraph 4 of the Notes provides that it is understood that the determination would be made at the end of the accounting period for which the distribution of profits takes place.

Paragraph 3

Paragraph 3 provides for exclusive residence country taxation (*i.e.,* an elimination of the source-country withholding tax) with respect to certain dividends paid by a company resident in one Contracting State to a resident in the other Contracting State. As described further below, the elimination of source-country withholding tax is available with respect to certain intercompany dividends and with respect to dividends received by tax-exempt pension funds.

Subparagraph (a) of paragraph 3 provides for the elimination of the source-country withholding tax on dividends paid by a company in one Contracting State in cases where the beneficial owner of the dividends is a company that is a resident of the other Contracting State, that has owned more than 50 percent of the voting power of the company paying the dividend for the 12-month period ending on the date on which entitlement to the dividends is determined, and that satisfies one of three certain additional conditions. The determination of whether the beneficial owner of the dividends owns more than 50 percent of the voting power of the paying company is made by taking into account stock owned both directly and stock owned indirectly through one or more residents of either Contracting State. For this purpose, stock owned through an entity will be treated as owned directly by the beneficiaries, members or participants of that entity to the extent that the income of the entity is treated as the income of such beneficiaries, members or participants under the laws of both Contracting States. To be eligible for the rule in subparagraph 3(a), the more-than 50 percent owner either (1) must meet the "publicly traded" test of subparagraph 1(c) of Article 22 (Limitation on Benefits), (2) must meet the "ownership-base erosion" *and* "active trade or business" tests described in subparagraph 1(f) and paragraph 2 of Article 22, or (3) must be granted such benefit with respect to subparagraph 3(a) of Article 10 by the competent authorities pursuant to paragraph 4 of Article 22.

These restrictions are necessary because of the increased pressure on the Limitation on Benefits tests resulting from the fact that the Convention is one of the few U.S. tax treaties to provide for the elimination of source-country withholding tax on intercompany dividends. The tests are intended to prevent companies from reorganizing in order to become eligible for the elimination of source-country withholding tax in circumstances where the Limitation on Benefits provision alone may not provide sufficient protection against treaty-shopping.

For example, assume that ThirdCo is a company resident in a third State. ThirdCo owns directly 100% of the issued and outstanding voting stock of USCo, a U.S. company, and of JCo, a Japanese company. JCo is a substantial company that manufactures consumer goods; USCo distributes such consumer goods in the United States. If ThirdCo contributes to JCo all the stock of USCo, dividends paid by USCo to JCo would satisfy the active trade or business test of paragraph 2 of Article 22. However, allowing ThirdCo to qualify for the exemption from withholding tax, which is not available to it under the third State's tax treaty (if any) with the United States, would encourage treaty-shopping.

In order to prevent this type of treaty-shopping, paragraph 3 requires JCo to meet the ownership-base erosion requirements of subparagraph 1(f) of Article 22 in addition to the active trade or business test of paragraph 2 of Article 22. Thus, JCo would not qualify for the exemption from withholding tax unless at least 50 percent of each class of its shares was owned by persons that are residents of Japan and eligible for treaty benefits under certain specified tests and less than 50 percent of JCo's gross income is paid in deductible payments to persons that are not residents of either Contracting State.

Alternatively, a company could obtain the benefit of the exemption from withholding tax if it met the publicly traded requirements of subparagraph 1(c) of Article 22 (or, as described below, is granted such benefit by the competent authorities pursuant to paragraph (4) of Article 22). It is not sufficient for a company to qualify for treaty benefits generally under the active trade or business test (paragraph 2 of Article 22) or the ownership-base erosion test (paragraph 1(f) of Article 22) unless it qualifies for treaty benefits under both.

If a company does not qualify for the exemption from source-country withholding tax under the publicly traded test or the ownership-base erosion *and* active trade or business tests, it may request a determination from the relevant competent authority pursuant to paragraph 4 of Article 22 (Limitation on Benefits) of the Convention. Benefits will be granted with respect to a dividend if the competent authority of the Contracting State in which the income arises determines that the establishment, acquisition or maintenance of such resident and the conduct of its operations did not have as one of its principal purposes the obtaining of benefits under the Convention.

Subparagraph (b) of paragraph 3 provides for exclusive taxation by the Contracting State of residence (*i.e.*, the elimination of source-country withholding tax) for dividends beneficially owned by a pension fund, as defined in subparagraph 1(m) of Article 3 (General Definitions), provided that such dividends are not derived from the carrying on of a business, directly or indirectly, by the pension fund.

Paragraph 4

Paragraph 4 provides rules for the treatment of dividends paid by a Regulated Investment Company (RIC) or a Real Estate Investment Trust (REIT) that are consistent with U.S. treaty policy.

The first sentence of paragraph 4 provides that dividends paid by a RIC or REIT are not eligible for the 5 percent maximum rate of withholding tax of subparagraph 2(a) or the elimination of source-country withholding tax of subparagraph 3(a).

The second sentence of paragraph 4 provides that the 10 percent maximum rate of withholding tax of subparagraph 2(b) applies to dividends paid by RICs and that the elimination of source-country withholding tax of subparagraph 3(b) applies to dividends paid by RICs and beneficially owned by a pension fund.

The third sentence of paragraph 4 provides that the 10 percent maximum rate of withholding tax also applies to dividends paid by a REIT, provided that one of three conditions is met. First, the dividend may qualify for the 10 percent maximum rate if the beneficial owner of the dividend is an individual or a pension fund holding an interest of not more than 10 percent in the REIT. Second, the dividend may qualify for the 10 percent maximum rate if it is paid with respect to a class of stock that is publicly traded and the beneficial owner of the dividend is a person holding an interest of not more than 5 percent of any class of the REIT's stock. Third, the dividend may qualify for the 10 percent maximum rate if the beneficial owner of the dividend holds an interest in the REIT of 10 percent or less and the REIT is "diversified." Paragraph 6 of the Protocol provides that a REIT is diversified if the gross value of no single interest in real property held by the REIT exceeds 10 percent of the gross value of the REIT's total interest in real property. Paragraph 6 of the Protocol also provides that, for purposes of this diversification test, foreclosure property is not considered an interest in real property, and a REIT holding a partnership interest is treated as owning its proportionate share of any interest in real property held by the partnership.

The restrictions set out above are intended to prevent the use of these entities to gain inappropriate U.S. tax benefits. For example, a company resident in Japan that wishes to hold a diversified portfolio of U.S. corporate shares could hold the portfolio directly and would bear a U.S. withholding tax of 10 percent on all of the dividends that it receives. Alternatively, it could hold the same diversified portfolio by purchasing 10 percent or more of the interests in a RIC. If the RIC is a pure conduit, there may be no U.S. tax cost to interposing the RIC in the chain of ownership. Absent the special rule in paragraph 4, such use of the RIC could transform portfolio dividends, taxable in the United States under the Convention at a 10 percent maximum rate of withholding tax, into direct investment dividends taxable at a 5 percent maximum rate of withholding tax or eligible for the elimination of source-country withholding tax.

Similarly, a resident of Japan directly holding U.S. real property would pay U.S. tax either at a 30 percent rate of withholding tax on the gross income or at graduated rates on the net income. As in the preceding example, by placing the real property in a REIT, the investor absent a special rule could transform real estate income into dividend income, taxable at the rates provided in Article 10, significantly reducing the U.S. tax that otherwise would be imposed. Paragraph 4 prevents this result and thereby avoids a disparity between the taxation of direct real estate investments and real estate investments made through REIT conduits. In the cases in which paragraph 4 allows a dividend from a REIT to be eligible for the 10 percent maximum rate of withholding tax, the holding in the REIT is not considered the equivalent of a direct holding in the underlying real property.

Paragraph 5

Paragraph 5 provides rules applicable to certain Japanese companies that are analogous to the rules of paragraph 4 applicable to U.S. RICs and REITS. Paragraph 5 is applicable to Japanese companies that are entitled to a deduction for dividends paid in computing taxable income in Japan. The treatment of dividends from such companies to U.S. residents raises the same concerns as the treatment of dividends from U.S. RICs or REITs to Japanese residents, and thus the same treatment is provided.

The first sentence of paragraph 5 provides that dividends paid by a company that is entitled to a deduction for dividends paid in computing its taxable income in Japan are not eligible for the 5 percent maximum rate of withholding tax of subparagraph 2(a) or the elimination of source-country withholding tax of subparagraph 3(a).

The second sentence of paragraph 5 provides that the 10 percent maximum rate of subparagraph 2(b) applies to dividends paid by such a company, provided that not more than 50 percent of the assets of the company consist, directly or indirectly, or real property situated in

Japan. The second sentence of paragraph 5 also provides that the elimination of source-country withholding tax of subparagraph 3(b) applies to dividends paid by such a company and beneficially owned by a pension fund, again provided that not more than 50 percent of the assets of the company consist, directly or indirectly, of real property situated in Japan. Thus, the second sentence of paragraph 5 is applicable to companies that are analogous to U.S. RICs, but not to U.S. REITs.

The third sentence of paragraph 5 is applicable to dividends paid by a company excluded from the second sentence – companies analogous to U.S. REITs. The 10 percent maximum rate of subparagraph (2)(b) applies to dividends paid by such a company if one of three conditions is met. First, the dividend may qualify for the 10 percent maximum rate if the beneficial owner of the dividend is an individual or a pension fund holding an interest of not more than 10 percent in the company. Second, the dividend may qualify for the 10 percent maximum rate if it is paid with respect to a class of interest in the company that is publicly traded and the beneficial owner of the dividend is a person holding an interest of not more than 5 percent of any class of interest in the company. Third, the dividend may qualify for the 10 percent maximum rate if the beneficial owner of the dividend holds an interest in the company of 10 percent or less and a company is "diversified." Paragraph 6 of the Protocol provides rules for determining whether a company is diversified. These rules are explained in the description of paragraph 4 above.

Paragraph 6

Paragraph 10 defines the term "dividends" broadly and is intended to cover all arrangements that yield a return on an equity investment in a corporation as determined in accordance with paragraph 2 of Article 3 (General Definitions) under the tax laws of the Contracting State of source, as well as arrangements that might be developed in the future.

The term "dividends" includes income from shares or other rights that are not treated as debt under the tax laws of the Contracting State of source and that participate in the profits of the company. The term also includes income that is subjected to the same tax treatment as income from shares by the tax laws of the Contracting State of source. Thus, a constructive dividend that results from a non-arm's length transaction between a corporation and a related party is a dividend, although the taxation of such an amount may be governed by the special rules provided in paragraph 8 of Article 11 (Interest), paragraph 4 of Article 12 (Royalties), and paragraph 3 of Article 21 (Other Income). Finally, a payment denominated as interest that is made by a thinly capitalized corporation may be treated as a dividend to the extent that the debt is recharacterized as equity under the laws of the Contracting State of source.

In the case of the United States, the term dividend includes amounts treated as a dividend under U.S. law upon the sale or redemption of shares or upon a transfer of shares in a reorganization. See, *e.g.*, Rev. Rul. 92-85, 1992-2 C.B. 69 (sale of foreign subsidiary's stock to U.S. sister company is a deemed dividend to extent of subsidiary's and sister's earnings and profits). Further, a distribution from a U.S. publicly traded limited partnership, which is taxed as a corporation under U.S. law, is a dividend for purposes of Article 10. However, a distribution by a limited liability company is not characterized by the United States as a dividend and, therefore, is not a dividend for purposes of Article 10, provided the limited liability company is not characterized as an association taxable as a corporation under U.S. law.

Paragraph 7

Paragraph 7 excludes from the general source country limitations under paragraph 2 and 3 dividends paid with respect to holdings that form part of the business property of a permanent establishment situated in the source country. Such dividends will be taxed on a net basis using the rates and rules of taxation generally applicable to residents of the Contracting State in which the permanent establishment is located, as modified by the Convention. An example of dividends paid with respect to the business property of a permanent establishment would be dividends derived by a dealer in stock or securities from stock or securities that the dealer held for sale to customers.

In the case of a permanent establishment that once existed in the Contracting State but that no longer exists, the provisions of paragraph 7 also apply, by virtue of paragraph 4 of the Protocol, to dividends that would be attributable to such a permanent establishment if it did exist in the year of payment or accrual. See the Technical Explanation of paragraph 1 of Article 7 (Business Profits).

Paragraph 8

The right of a Contracting State to tax dividends paid by a company that is a resident of the other Contracting State is restricted by paragraph 8 to cases in which the dividends are paid to a resident of that Contracting State or are attributable to a permanent establishment in that Contracting State. Thus, a Contracting State may not impose a "secondary" withholding tax on dividends paid by a nonresident company out of earnings and profits from that Contracting State. In the case of the United States, paragraph 8, therefore, does not permit the imposition of taxes under sections 871 and 882(a) on dividends paid by foreign corporations that have a U.S. source under section 861(a)(2)(B).

The paragraph also restricts the right of a Contracting State to impose corporate level taxes on undistributed profits, other than a branch profits tax described in paragraph 9. The accumulated earnings tax and the personal holding company taxes are Federal income taxes and therefore are taxes covered in Article 2 (Taxes Covered). Accordingly, under the provisions of Article 7 (Business Profits), the United States may not impose those taxes on the income of a resident of the other State except to the extent that income is attributable to a permanent establishment in the United States. Paragraph 8 further confirms the restriction on the U.S. authority to impose those taxes. The paragraph does not restrict the right of a Contracting State to tax its resident shareholders on undistributed earnings of a corporation resident in the other Contracting State. Thus, the U.S. authority to impose the foreign personal holding company tax, its taxes on subpart F income and on an increase in earnings invested in U.S. property, and its tax on income of a passive foreign investment company that is a qualified electing fund is in no way restricted by this provision.

Paragraph 9

Paragraph 9 permits a Contracting State to impose a branch profits tax on a company resident in the other Contracting State. The tax is in addition to other taxes permitted by the Convention. The term "company" is defined in subparagraph 1(f) Article 3 (General Definitions).

A Contracting State may impose a branch profits tax on a company if the company has income attributable to a permanent establishment in that Contracting State, derives income from real property in that Contracting State that is taxed on a net basis under Article 6 (Income from Real Property), or realizes gains taxable in that State under paragraph 1 of Article 13 (Gains). The imposition of such tax is limited, however, to the portion of the aforementioned items of income that represents the amount of such income that is equivalent to the amount of dividends that would have been paid if such activities had been conducted in a separate legal entity.

Paragraph 7 of the Protocol provides that the amount of such income that is equivalent to the amount of dividends that would have been paid if such activities had been conducted in a separate legal entity shall be, for any taxable year, the after-tax earnings from the company's activities described in paragraph 9, adjusted to take into account changes in the company's investment in the Contracting State imposing the branch profits tax. This amount approximates the dividend that a branch office would have paid during the year if the branch had been operated as a separate subsidiary company, and thus is consistent with the relevant rules under the U.S. branch profits tax. Generally, those rules impose a tax on an amount for a particular year that is equivalent to the income described above that is included in the corporation's effectively connected earnings and profits for that year, after payment of the corporate tax under Articles 6 (Income from Real Property), 7 (Business Profits) or 13 (Gains), reduced for any increase in the branch's U.S. net equity during the year or increased for any reduction in its U.S. net equity during the year. U.S. net equity is U.S. assets less U.S. liabilities. See Treas. Reg. section 1.884-1. The United States may not impose its branch profits tax on the business profits of a corporation resident in Japan that are effectively connected with a U.S. trade or business but that are not attributable to a permanent establishment and are not otherwise subject to U.S. taxation under Article 6 (Income from Real Property) or paragraph 1 of Article 13 (Gains).

Japan currently does not impose a branch profits tax. If Japan were to impose such a tax, the base of such a tax would be limited to an amount described in paragraph 7 of the Protocol and therefore analogous to the base of the U.S. branch profits tax.

The branch profits tax will not be imposed, however, if certain requirements are met. In general, these requirements provide rules for a branch that parallel the rules for when a dividend paid by a subsidiary will be subject to exclusive residence-country taxation (i.e., the elimination of source-country withholding tax). Accordingly, the branch profits tax may not be imposed in the case of a company that (1) meets the "publicly traded" "test of subparagraph 1(c) of Article 22 (Limitation on Benefits), (2) meets the "ownership-base erosion" *and* "active trade or business" tests described in subparagraph 1(f) and paragraph 2 of Article 22, or (3) is granted such benefit with respect to the branch profits tax by the competent authorities pursuant to paragraph 4 of Article 22.

Thus, for example, if a Japanese company would be subject to the branch profits tax with respect to profits attributable to a U.S. branch and not reinvested in that branch, paragraph 9 may apply to eliminate the branch profits tax if the company either met the "publicly traded" test or met both the "ownership-base erosion" *and* "active trade or business" tests. If, by contrast, a Japanese company that did not meet those tests, then the branch profits tax would apply, unless the Japanese company is granted benefits with respect to the elimination of the branch profits tax by the competent authorities pursuant to paragraph 4 of Article 22.

Paragraph 10

Paragraph 10 provides that the branch profits tax permitted by paragraph 9 shall not be imposed at a rate of withholding tax exceeding the maximum direct investment dividend rate of withholding tax of 5 percent. This rule will apply only if the conditions for exemption from the branch profits tax described above under paragraph 9 are not met.

Paragraph 11

Paragraph 11 provides that a resident of a Contracting State shall not be considered the beneficial owner of dividends in respect of preferred stock in certain "back-to-back" preferred stock arrangements. The benefits of Article 10 therefore are not available with respect to such dividends. This rule is similar to rules dealing with interest, royalties, and other income in paragraph 11 of Article 11 (Interest), paragraph 5 of Article 12 (Royalties), and paragraph 4 of Article 21 (Other Income).

Collectively, these limited "anti-conduit" rules are significantly narrower than similar rules that are provided under U.S. domestic law, including in particular the rules of regulation section 1.881-3 and other regulations adopted under the authority of section 7701(l) of the Code. The limited anti-conduit rules provided in the Convention are not included in the U.S. Model, but are included here at the request of Japan in order to ensure that Japan can prevent residents of third countries from improperly obtaining the benefits of the Convention in certain limited circumstances. For Japan, these transaction-based anti-abuse rules are a necessary supplement to the entity-based anti-treaty shopping rules in Article 22 (Limitation on Benefits) and Japanese domestic law, which does not include rules such as the anti-conduit rules of Code section 7701(l) and regulation section 1.881-3. On the other hand, U.S. domestic law provides specific anti-conduit rules, as well as a number of other domestic anti-abuse principles (such as the business purpose doctrine) that apply in the treaty context. The United States intends that the inclusion of the limited anti-conduit rules in particular articles of the Convention shall create no negative inference regarding the application of U.S. domestic anti-abuse rules (*e.g.*, the anti-conduit rules and other anti-abuse rules referred to above) to those articles, other articles of the Convention, or other U.S. tax treaties.

Paragraph 11 in particular provides that a resident of a Contracting State shall not be considered the beneficial owner of dividends in respect of preferred stock if such preferred stock would not have been established or acquired unless a person that is not entitled to the same or more favorable treaty benefits and that is not a resident of either Contracting State held equivalent preferred stock in the resident. The operation of this rule can be illustrated in the following examples:

Example 1. A, a U.S. resident, owns preferred stock in X, a Japanese company, that entitles A to dividends of 10x each year to the extent of X's earnings. B, a resident of a third country that does not have a tax treaty with Japan, owns preferred stock in A that entitles B to dividends of 10x each year to the extent of A's earnings and otherwise has terms that are equivalent to the terms of the preferred stock of X held by A. A would not have established or acquired its preferred stock in X if B did not hold preferred stock in A. X has earnings of 15x in year one, and pays a dividend of 10x to A. A pays a dividend of 10x to B. Under paragraph 11, A will not be considered the beneficial owner of the dividends from X, and therefore is not entitled to treaty benefits with respect to the dividends from X.

Example 2. The facts are the same as the facts of Example 1, except that, instead of owning preferred stock in A, B holds a debt claim against A that entitles B to interest of 10x each year. A pays interest of 10x to B. Paragraph 11 does not apply to deny treaty benefits to A with respect to the dividends from X.

No inference is intended as to the result of Example 2 in cases of dividends from U.S. companies under U.S. domestic anti-abuse rules (*e.g.*, the anti-conduit rules and other anti-abuse rules referred to above).

Relation to Other Articles

Notwithstanding the foregoing limitations on source country taxation of dividends, the saving clause of subparagraph 4(a) of Article 1 (General Scope) permits the United States to tax dividends received by its residents and citizens, subject to the special foreign tax credit rules of paragraph 3 of Article 23 (Relief from Double Taxation), as if the Convention had not come into effect.

The benefits of this Article are also subject to the provisions of Article 22 (Limitation on Benefits). Thus, if a resident of Japan is the beneficial owner of dividends paid by a U.S. company, the shareholder must qualify for treaty benefits under at least one of the tests of Article 22 in order to receive the benefits of this Article.

Article 11 (Interest)

Article 11 provides rules for the taxation of interest arising in one Contracting State and paid to a beneficial owner that is a resident of the other Contracting State.

Paragraph 1

Paragraph 1 generally grants to the Contracting State of residence the non-exclusive right to tax interest which arises in the other Contracting State and paid to its residents.

Paragraph 2

Paragraph 2 provides that the Contracting State in which the interest arises may also tax the interest, but if the beneficial owner of the interest is a resident of the other Contracting State, the rate of tax shall not exceed 10 percent of the gross amount of the interest.

The term "beneficial owner" is not defined in the Convention, and is, therefore, defined under the internal law of the Contracting State of source. The beneficial owner of the interest for purposes of Article 11 is the person to which the interest income is attributable for tax purposes under the laws of the Contracting State of source. Thus, if interest arising in a Contracting State is received by a nominee or agent that is a resident of the other Contracting State on behalf of a person that is not a resident of that other Contracting State, the interest is not entitled to the benefits of Article 11. However, interest received by a nominee on behalf of a resident of that other State would be entitled to benefits. These limitations are confirmed by paragraph 8 of the OECD Commentary to Article 11. See also paragraph 24 of the OECD Commentary to Article 1.

Paragraph 3

Paragraph 3 provides for exclusive residence based taxation (*i.e.*, an elimination of source-country withholding tax) in certain cases.

Under subparagraph (a), interest beneficially owned by a Contracting State, a political subdivision or a local authority thereof (i.e., in the United States a State or local government), the central bank of that Contracting State or any institution wholly owned by that Contracting State is subject to exclusive residence based taxation. Paragraph 4 provides a list of institutions in the case of Japan and the United States described by the terms "the central bank" and "institution wholly owned by a Contracting State." In the case of Japan, these terms include the Bank of Japan, the Japan Bank for International Cooperation, and the Nippon Export and Investment Insurance. In the case of the United States, these terms include the Federal Reserve Banks, the U.S. Export-Import Bank, and the Overseas Private Investment Corporation. Paragraph 4 also provides that this list can be expanded to other financial institutions wholly owned by a Contracting State by agreement between the Governments of the Contracting States through an exchange of diplomatic notes.

Subparagraph (b) provides for exclusive residence based taxation for interest beneficially owned by a resident of a Contracting State with respect to debt-claims backed by that Contracting State or other governmental institutions referred to in subparagraph (a). Interest beneficially owned by a resident of a Contracting State with respect to debt-claims guaranteed, insured or indirectly financed by the Contracting State, a political subdivision or a local authority thereof, the central bank of that Contracting State or any institution wholly owned by that Contracting State (as defined in paragraph 4) is subject to exclusive residence based taxation.

Subparagraph (c) provides that interest beneficially owned by certain financial institutions resident in a Contracting State is subject to exclusive residence based taxation. In particular, exclusive residence based taxation is provided for interest beneficially owned by a bank, including an investment bank, an insurance company, or a registered securities dealer. Exclusive residence based taxation also is provided for interest beneficially owned by any other enterprise, provided that in the three taxable years preceding the taxable year in which the interest is paid, the enterprise derives more than 50 percent of its liabilities from the issuance of bonds in the financial markets or from taking deposits at interest, and more than 50 percent of the assets of the enterprise consists of debt-claims against persons that are not related to the resident under the standard provided in subparagraph (a) or (b) of paragraph 1 of Article 9 (Associated Enterprises). Thus, non-bank financial institutions such as commercial finance companies or consumer credit companies are covered by this exemption provided that they obtain more than half of their borrowed funds by borrowing from the public.

Paragraph 5 of the Notes provides that the term "bonds" includes bonds, commercial paper, and medium-term notes, whether collateralized or not, and provides that bonds that are subject to transfer restrictions applicable to private placements generally shall not be considered to have been issued in the financial markets. However, offerings qualifying for exemption from securities registration requirements pursuant to Rule 144A promulgated under the Securities Act of 1933 shall not be considered subject to transfer restrictions applicable to private placements, and thus generally shall be considered to have been issued in the financial markets.

It is understood that the asset test and the liability test may be applied on the basis of the average of the assets and liabilities, respectively, of the enterprise at the end of each of the three years preceding the taxable year in which the interest is paid. Thus, for example, if an enterprise derives from the issuance of bonds in the financial markets 30 percent of its liabilities in year 1, 60 percent of its liabilities in year 2, and 70 percent of its liabilities in year 3, then it will be treated as deriving more than 50 percent of its liabilities from the issuance of bonds in the financial markets in the three taxable years preceding year 4.

Subparagraph (d) provides for exclusive taxation by the Contracting State of residence for interest beneficially owned by a pension fund, as defined in subparagraph 1(m) of Article 3 (General Definitions), provided that such dividends are not derived from the carrying on of a business, directly or indirectly, by the pension fund.

Subparagraph (e) provides that interest beneficially owned by a resident of a Contracting State and paid with respect to indebtedness arising as a part of a sale by that resident of equipment or merchandise is subject to exclusive residence based taxation.

Paragraph 4

Paragraph 4 provides a list of institutions described by the terms "the central bank" and "institution wholly owned by a Contracting State", as used in subparagraphs (a) and (b) of paragraph 3, for purposes of paragraph 3. This list is described in the explanation to paragraph 3, above.

Paragraph 5

The term "interest" as used in Article 11 is defined in paragraph 5 to include, *inter alia*, income from debt claims of every kind, whether or not secured by a mortgage and whether or not carrying a right to participate in the debtor's profits. The term does not, however, include amounts that are treated as dividends under Article 10 (Dividends).

The term interest also includes amounts subject to the same tax treatment as income from money lent under the law of the State in which the income arises. Thus, for purposes of the Convention, amounts that the United States will treat as interest include (i) the difference between the issue price and the stated redemption price at maturity of a debt instrument (*i.e.*, original issue discount ("OID")), which may be wholly or partially realized on the disposition of a debt instrument (section 1273), (ii) amounts that are imputed interest on a deferred sales contract (section 483), (iii) amounts treated as interest or OID under the stripped bond rules (section 1286), (iv) amounts treated as original issue discount under the below-market interest rate rules (section 7872), (v) a partner's distributive share of a partnership's interest income (section 702), (vi) the interest portion of periodic payments made under a "finance lease" or similar contractual arrangement that in substance is a borrowing by the nominal lessee to finance the acquisition of property, (vii) amounts included in the income of a holder of a residual interest in a REMIC (section 860E), because these amounts generally are subject to the same taxation treatment as interest under U.S. tax law, and (viii) interest with respect to notional principal contracts that are recharacterized as loans because of a "substantial non-periodic payment."

Paragraph 6

Paragraph 6 provides an exception to paragraphs 1, 2, and 3 where the beneficial owner of the interest carries on business through a permanent establishment in the Contracting State in which the interest arises and the interest is attributable to that permanent establishment. In such cases, the applicable provisions of Article 7 (Business Profits) will apply.

The provisions of paragraph 4 of the Protocol apply to income described in this paragraph. For example, interest income that is attributable to a permanent establishment and that accrues during the existence of the permanent establishment, but is received after the permanent establishment no longer exists, remains taxable under the provisions of Article 7 (Business Profits), and not under this Article.

Paragraph 7

Paragraph 7 provides a source rule that is similar to the interest source rule of the prior Convention. Interest generally is considered to arise in a Contracting State when paid by a resident of that Contracting State. Special rules are provided where the interest is borne by a permanent establishment of the person paying the interest. In such a case, if the permanent establishment is situated in a Contracting State, then the interest shall be deemed to arise in that Contracting State; and if the permanent establishment is situated in a state other than the Contracting States, then the interest shall not be deemed to arise in either Contracting State. While interest borne by a permanent establishment that is situated in a state other than the

Contracting States thus will not be eligible for the benefits of the Convention, it may be eligible for the benefits of the tax treaty, if any, between the state in which the permanent establishment is situated and the Contracting State of which the beneficial owner of the interest is a resident.

For purposes of paragraph 7, interest is considered to be borne by a permanent establishment if it is allocable to taxable income of that permanent establishment or fixed base. If the actual amount of interest on the books of a U.S. branch of a resident of Japan exceeds the amount of interest allocated to the branch under Treas. Reg. Section 1.882-5, the amount of such excess will not be considered U.S. source interest for purposes of this Article.

Paragraph 8

Paragraph 8 provides that, in cases involving special relationships between persons, Article 11 applies only to that portion of the total interest payments between those persons that would have been made absent such special relationships (*i.e.*, an arm's-length interest payment). The term "special relationship" is not defined in the Convention. In applying this paragraph, the United States considers the term to include the relationships described in Article 9 (Associated Enterprises), which in turn correspond to the definition of "control" for purposes of section 482 of the Code. This is consistent with paragraph 33 of the Commentary to Article 11 of the OECD Model.

Paragraph 8 also provides that any amount of interest paid in excess of the amount that would be been paid absent a special relationship may be taxable in the Contracting State in which it arises at a rate not to exceed 5 percent. This rule is similar to rules provided in paragraph 4 of Article 12 (Royalties), and paragraph 3 of Article 21 (Other Income), which provide that any amount paid in excess of the amount that would have been paid absent a special relationship may be taxable in the Contracting State in which they arise at a rate not to exceed 5 percent.

The Convention's treatment of such excess amounts is consistent in most circumstances with the results under the U.S. Model and U.S. domestic law and practice. Absent the specific rule in the Convention, in most cases the United States would treat such excess amounts as a dividend or as a contribution to capital, depending on the relationship between the parties, and tax such amounts accordingly. Under the Convention, a maximum 5 percent withholding tax rate generally applies to dividends where the beneficial owner is a company owning directly or indirectly at least 10 percent of the voting stock of the company paying the dividends. In Japan, the general practice in the context of investment income such as interest, dividends, or other income is to impose withholding taxes on the amount in excess of the arm's length amount at the domestic rate. Thus, for example, if a Japanese company makes an interest payment to its non-Japanese parent company, and Japan determines that the amount of the interest payment exceeded an arm's-length amount, Japan will deny a deduction for the excess amount and treat the excess amount as an interest payment subject to the appropriate withholding rate applicable to interest paid by Japanese companies under its domestic law, which is generally 20 percent. Under the Convention, such excess amounts instead are subject to a maximum 5 percent rate of withholding taxes.

Paragraph 8 does not address cases where, owing to a special relationship between the payer and the beneficial owner, or between both of them and some other person, the amount of the interest is less than an arm's-length amount. In those cases a transaction may be characterized to reflect its substance and interest may be imputed consistent with the definition of interest in paragraph 5. Consistent with Article 9 (Associated Enterprises), the United States would apply section 482 or 7872 of the Code to determine the amount of imputed interest in those cases.

Paragraph 9

Paragraph 9 provides an anti-abuse exception to paragraphs 2 and 3 for excess inclusions from entities used to securitize real estate mortgages or other assets. Sub-paragraph (b) serves as a backstop to Code section 860G(b). That section generally requires that a foreign person holding a residual interest in a real estate mortgage investment conduit ("REMIC") take into account for U.S. tax purposes "any excess inclusion" and "amounts includible...[under the REMIC provisions] when paid or distributed (or when the interest is disposed of)...."

Without a full tax at source, non-U.S. transferees of residual interests would have a competitive advantage over U.S. transferees at the time these interests are initially offered. Absent this rule, there would be a potential for inappropriate results with respect to mortgages held in a REMIC because of opportunities for tax avoidance created by differences in the timing of taxable and economic income produced by such interests. In many cases, the transfer to the foreign person is simply disregarded under Reg. § 1.860G-3. Paragraph 9 also serves to indicate that excess inclusions from REMICs are not considered "other income" subject to Article 21 (Other Income).

Paragraph 9 is analogous to subparagraph 5(b) of the U.S. Model, except that in the Convention the provision is drafted to apply bilaterally. Thus, for example, paragraph 9 does not refer to the long-term Federal rate used to determine the amount of an excess inclusion, but rather to "the return on comparable debt instruments as specified by the domestic law of that Contracting State." Nevertheless, for U.S. tax purposes, the tax imposed "to the extent that the amount of interest paid exceeds the return on comparable debt instruments as specified by the domestic law of that Contracting State" is the withholding tax that would be imposed upon an excess inclusion with respect to a residual interest in a REMIC under section 860G(b).

Unlike the U.S. model, the Convention does not contain a specific provision applicable to so-called "contingent interest." Under the U.S. Model, which generally exempts interest from source-based taxation (i.e., provides for a zero rate of withholding tax on interest), certain contingent interest that is paid by a resident of one of the Contracting States to a resident of the other Contracting State may be taxed at a rate not exceeding the highest rate applicable to dividend income. This rule is not included in the Convention because the highest rate applicable to dividend income (10 percent, as prescribed in paragraph 2 of Article 10 (Dividends)) is the same as the general rate applicable to interest income (10 percent, as prescribed in paragraph 2 of Article 11 (Interest)).

Paragraph 10

Paragraph 10 permits a Contracting State to impose its branch level interest tax on a corporation resident in the other Contracting State. The base of this tax is the excess, if any, of the interest deductible in the first-mentioned Contracting State in computing the profits of the corporation that are subject to tax in the first-mentioned Contracting State and either attributable to a permanent establishment in the first-mentioned Contracting State or subject to tax in the first-mentioned Contracting State under Article 6 or Article 13 of this Convention over the interest paid by or from the permanent establishment or trade or business in the first-mentioned Contracting State. Such excess interest may be taxed as if it were interest arising in the first-mentioned Contracting State and beneficially owned by the corporation resident in the other Contracting State. Thus, such excess interest may be taxed by the Contracting State of source at a rate not to exceed the 10 percent rate provided for in paragraph 2, and shall be exempt from tax by the Contracting State of source if the recipient corporation is described in paragraph 3.

Paragraph 11

Paragraph 11 provides that a resident of a Contracting State shall not be considered the beneficial owner of interest in certain "back-to-back" loan arrangements. The benefits of Article 11 therefore are not available with respect to such interest. This rule is similar to rules dealing with interest, royalties, and other income in paragraph 11 of Article 10 (Dividends), paragraph 5 of Article 12 (Royalties), and paragraph 4 of Article 21 (Other Income). These limited "anti-conduit" rules and their interaction with U.S. domestic law are discussed in the explanation of paragraph 11 of Article 10 above.

Paragraph 11 in particular provides that a resident of a Contracting State shall not be considered the beneficial owner of interest in respect of a debt-claim if such debt-claim would not have been established unless a person that is not entitled to the same or more favorable treaty benefits and that is not a resident of either Contracting State held an equivalent debt claim in the resident. The operation of this rule can be illustrated in the following examples:

Example 1. A, a U.S. resident, holds a debt-claim against X, a Japanese company, that entitles A to interest of 10x each year. B, a resident of a third country that does not have a tax treaty with Japan, owns a debt-claim against A that entitles B to interest of 10x each year and otherwise has terms that are equivalent to the terms of the debt-claim held by A. A would not have established its debt-claim against X if B did not hold a debt-claim against A. X pays interest of 10x to A, which pays interest of 10x to B. Under paragraph 11, A will not be considered the beneficial owner of the interest from X, and therefore is not entitled to treaty benefits with respect to the interest from X.

Example 2. The facts are the same as the facts of Example 1, except that, instead of owning a debt-claim against A, B holds preferred stock in A that entitles B to 10x each year to the extent of A's earnings in that year. A pays dividends of 10x to B. Paragraph 11 does not apply to deny treaty benefits to A with respect to the interest from X.

No inference is intended as to the result of Example 2 in cases of interest arising in the United States under U.S. domestic anti-abuse rules (*e.g.*, the anti-conduit rules and other anti-abuse rules referred to in the explanation of paragraph 11 of Article 10 (Dividends)).

Relation to Other Articles

Notwithstanding the foregoing limitations on source country taxation of interest, the saving clause of subparagraph 4(a) of Article 1 (General Scope) permits the United States to tax its residents and citizens, subject to the special foreign tax credit rules of paragraph 3 of Article 23 (Relief from Double Taxation), as if the Convention had not come into force.

The benefits of this Article are also subject to the provisions of Article 22 (Limitation on Benefits). Thus, if a resident of Japan is the beneficial owner of interest paid by a U.S. corporation, the resident must qualify for treaty benefits under at least one of the tests of Article 22 in order to receive the benefits of this Article.

Article 12 (Royalties)

Article 12 provides rules for the taxation of royalties arising in one Contracting State and paid to a beneficial owner that is a resident of the other Contracting State.

Paragraph 1

Paragraph 1 generally grants to the Contracting State of residence the exclusive right to tax royalties (i.e., an elimination of source-country withholding tax) beneficially owned by its residents and arising in the other Contracting State.

The term "beneficially owned" is not defined in the Convention, and is, therefore, defined under the internal law of the Contracting State of source. The person that beneficially owns the royalty for purposes of Article 12 is the person to which the royalty income is attributable for tax purposes under the laws of the State of source. Thus, if a royalty arising in a Contracting State is received by a nominee or agent that is a resident of the other State on behalf of a person that is not a resident of that other Contracting State, the royalty is not entitled to the benefits of Article 12. However, a royalty received by a nominee on behalf of a resident of that other State would be entitled to benefits. These limitations are confirmed by paragraph 4 of the OECD Commentary to Article 12. See also paragraph 24 of the OECD Commentary to Article 1.

Paragraph 2

Paragraph 2 defines the term "royalties," as used in Article 12, to include any consideration for the use of, or the right to use, any copyright of literary, artistic, scientific or other work; for the use of, or the right to use, any patent, trademark, design or model, plan, secret formula or process, or other like right or property; or for information concerning industrial, commercial, or scientific experience. The term "royalties" does not include gain derived from the alienation of any right or property that would give rise to royalties, whether or not such gain is contingent on the productivity, use, or further alienation thereof. Such gains are dealt with under Article 13 (Gains), and therefore generally are subject to the same treatment under the Convention as royalties. The term "royalties" also does not include income from leasing personal property.

The term royalties is defined in the Convention and therefore is generally independent of domestic law. Certain terms used in the definition are not defined in the Convention, but these may be defined under domestic tax law. For example, the term "secret process or formulas" is found in the Code, and its meaning has been elaborated in the context of sections 351 and 367. See Rev. Rul. 55- 17, 1955-1 C.B. 388; Rev. Rul. 64-56, 1964-1 C.B. 133; Rev. Proc. 69- 19, 1969-2 C.B. 301.

Consideration for the use or right to use cinematographic films and films or tapes for radio or television broadcasting is specifically included in the definition of royalties. It is intended that, with respect to any subsequent technological advances in the field of radio or television broadcasting, consideration received for the use of such technology will also be included in the definition of royalties.

If an artist who is resident in one Contracting State records a performance in the other Contracting State, retains a copyrighted interest in a recording, and receives payments for the right to use the recording based on the sale or public playing of the recording, then the right of such other Contracting State to tax those payments is governed by Article 12. See Boulez v. Commissioner, 83 T.C. 584 (1984), aff'd, 810 F.2d 209 (D.C. Cir. 1986). By contrast, if the artist earns in the other Contracting State income covered by Article 16 (Artistes and Sportsmen), for example, endorsement income from the artist's attendance at a film screening, and if such income also is attributable to one of the rights described in Article 12 (*e.g.*, the use of the artist's photograph in promoting the screening), Article 16 and not Article 12 is applicable to such income.

Computer software generally is protected by copyright laws around the world. Under the Convention, consideration received for the use of, or the right to use, computer software is treated either as royalties or as business profits, depending on the facts and circumstances of the transaction giving rise to the payment. Because computer software is protected by copyright laws, consideration received for the use of, or the right to use, computer software may be treated as royalties notwithstanding the fact that the term "computer software" is not used in paragraph 2.

The primary factor in determining whether consideration received for the use of, or the right to use, computer software is treated as royalties or as business profits is the nature of the rights transferred. See Treas. Reg. section 1.861-18. The fact that the transaction is characterized as a license for copyright law purposes is not dispositive. For example, a typical retail sale of "shrink wrap" software generally will not be considered to give rise to royalty income, even though for copyright law purposes it may be characterized as a license.

The means by which the computer software is transferred are not relevant for purposes of the analysis. Consequently, if software is electronically transferred but the rights obtained by the transferee are substantially equivalent to rights in a program copy, the payment will be considered business profits.

The term "industrial, commercial, or scientific experience" (sometimes referred to as "know-how") has the meaning ascribed to it in paragraph 11 of the Commentary to Article 12 of the OECD Model. Consistent with that meaning, the term may include information that is ancillary to a right otherwise giving rise to royalties, such as a patent or secret process.

Know-how also may include, in limited cases, technical information that is conveyed through technical or consultancy services. It does not include general educational training of the user's employees, nor does it include information developed especially for the user, such as a technical plan or design developed according to the user's specifications. Thus, as provided in paragraph 11 of the Commentary to Article 12 of the OECD Model, the term "royalties" does not include payments received as consideration for after-sales service, for services rendered by a seller to a purchaser under a guarantee, or for pure technical assistance.

The term "royalties" also does not include payments for professional services (such as architectural, engineering, legal, managerial, medical, software development services). For example, income from the design of a refinery by an engineer (even if the engineer employed know-how in the process of rendering the design) or the production of a legal brief by a lawyer is not income from the transfer of know-how taxable under Article 12, but is income from services taxable under either Article 7 (Business Profits) or Article 14 (Income from Employment). Professional services may be embodied in property that gives rise to royalties, however. Thus, if a professional contracts to develop patentable property and retains rights in the resulting property under the development contract, subsequent license payments made for those rights would be royalties.

Paragraph 3

Paragraph 3 provides an exception to the rules of paragraph 1 that eliminate source country taxation of royalties. This paragraph applies in cases where the beneficial owner of the royalties carries on business through a permanent establishment in the Contracting State of source and the royalties are attributable to that permanent establishment. In such cases the provisions of Article 7 (Business Profits) will apply.

The provisions of paragraph 7 of Article 7 (Business Profits) apply to income described in this paragraph. For example, royalty income that is attributable to a permanent establishment and that accrues during the existence of the permanent establishment, but is received after the permanent establishment no longer exists, remains taxable under the provisions of Article 7 (Business Profits), and not under this Article.

Paragraph 4

Paragraph 4 provides that in cases involving special relationships between the payer and beneficial owner of royalties, Article 12 applies only to the extent the royalties would have been paid absent such special relationships (*i.e.*, an arm's-length royalty). Any excess amount of royalties paid may be taxable in the Contracting State in which it arises at a rate not to exceed 5 percent. An explanation of this rule is provided in the explanation of paragraph 8 of Article 11 (Interest), above.

Paragraph 5

Paragraph 5 provides that a resident of a Contracting State shall not be considered the beneficial owner of royalties in certain "back-to-back" royalty arrangements. The benefits of Article 12 therefore are not available with respect to such royalties. This rule is similar to rules dealing with interest, royalties, and other income in paragraph 11 of Article 10 (Dividends), paragraph 11 of Article 11 (Interest), and paragraph 4 of Article 21 (Other Income). These limited "anti-conduit" rules and their interaction with U.S. domestic law are discussed in the explanation of paragraph 11 of Article 10 above.

Paragraph 5 in particular provides that a resident of a Contracting State shall not be considered the beneficial owner of royalties in respect of intangible property if such royalties would not have been paid unless the resident pays royalties in respect of the same intangible property to a person that is not entitled to the same or more favorable treaty benefits and that is not a resident of either Contracting State. The operation of this rule can be illustrated in the following examples:

Example 1. B, a resident of a third country that does not have a tax treaty with Japan, licenses Japanese patent rights to A. A sublicenses its entire interest in the same Japanese patent rights to X, a Japanese company. X pays royalties of 100x to A with respect to the sublicense, and A pays royalties of 99x to B with respect to the license. The 100x of royalties would not have been paid to A if A had not paid royalties with respect to the Japanese patent rights to B. Under paragraph 5, A will not be considered the beneficial owner of the royalties from X, and therefore is not entitled to treaty benefits with respect to the royalties from X.

Example 2. The facts are the same as the facts of Example 1, except that B holds a debt claim against A that entitles B to 99x each year to the extent of A's earnings in that year. A pays interest of 99x to B. Paragraph 5 does not apply to deny treaty benefits to A with respect to the royalties from X.

No inference is intended as to the result of Example 2 in cases of interest arising in the United States under U.S. domestic anti-abuse rules (*e.g.*, the anti-conduit rules and other anti-abuse rules referred to in the explanation of paragraph 11 of Article 10 (Dividends)).

Relation to Other Articles

Notwithstanding the foregoing limitations on source country taxation of royalties, the saving clause of subparagraph 4(a) of Article 1 (General Scope) permits the United States to tax its residents and citizens, subject to the special foreign tax credit rules of paragraph 3 of Article 23 (Relief from Double Taxation), as if the Convention had not come into force.

The benefits of this Article are also subject to the provisions of Article 22 (Limitation on Benefits). Thus, if a resident of Japan is the beneficial owner of royalties paid by a U.S. corporation, the shareholder must qualify for treaty benefits under at least one of the tests of Article 22 in order to receive the benefits of this Article.

Article 13 (Gains)

Article 13 assigns either primary or exclusive taxing jurisdiction over gains from the alienation of property to the Contracting State of residence or the Contracting State of source and defines the terms necessary to apply the Article.

Paragraph 1

Paragraph 1 preserves the non-exclusive right of the Contracting State of source to tax gains attributable to the alienation of real property (as defined in paragraph 2 of Article 6 (Real Property)) situated in that Contracting State. Paragraph 9 of the Protocol provides that distributions made by a REIT are taxable under paragraph 1 of Article 13 (not under Article 10 (Dividends)) when they are attributable to gains derived from the alienation of real property.

Paragraph 1 of this Article, in combination with paragraph 2 of this Article, permits the United States to apply section 897 of the Code to tax gains derived by a resident of Japan that are attributable to the alienation of real property situated in the United States, as well as gains attributable to the alienation of shares in certain real property holding companies.

Paragraph 2

Paragraph 2 preserves the non-exclusive right of the Contracting State of source to tax gains from the indirect alienation of real property situated in that Contracting State through the alienation of entities that hold an interest in real property by residents of the other Contracting State.

Subparagraph (a) preserves the non-exclusive right of the Contracting State of source to tax gains from the alienation of shares in a company that is a resident of that Contracting State and derives at least 50 percent of its value directly or indirectly from real property situated in that Contracting State. Gains from the alienation of shares which are part of a class of shares which are traded on a recognized stock exchange and of which the alienator (and persons thereto) own in the aggregate 5 percent or less are not taxable by the Contracting State of source. This paragraph thus permits the United States to tax U.S. real property holding companies under its domestic law. See I.R.C. § 897(c).

Subparagraph (b) preserves the non-exclusive right of the Contracting State of source to tax gains from the alienation of an interest in a partnership, trust or estate to the extent that its assets consist of real property situated in that Contracting State.

Paragraph 3

Paragraph 3 preserves the non-exclusive right of the Contracting State of source to tax gains from the alienation of shares in a financial institution that is a resident of that Contracting State in certain narrow circumstances. In general, paragraph 3 is applicable only where: (1) a Contracting State provides, pursuant to the domestic law concerning failure resolution involving imminent insolvency of financial institutions, substantial financial assistance to a financial institution that is a resident in that Contracting State; (2) a resident of the other Contracting State acquires shares in the financial institution from the first-mentioned Contracting State; and (3) the resident of the other Contracting State alienates shares within five years from the first date on which such financial assistance was provided. In such a case, under subparagraph 3(a) the first-mentioned Contracting State may tax gains derived by the resident of the other Contracting State on the alienation of such shares.

Subparagraph 3(b) provides a transition rule under which the rule of subparagraph 3(a) is not applicable if the resident of the other Contracting State acquired any shares in the financial institution before the entry into force of the Convention or pursuant to a binding contracting entered into before the entry into force of the Convention. This transition rule is intended to preserve the expectations of residents of one Contracting State that had made investments prior to the entry into force of the Convention in financial institutions that are residents of the other Contracting State. This transition rule also allows residents to protect their investments in a financial institution acquired before the entry into force of the Convention by purchasing additional shares in that financial institution after the entry into force of the Convention. Thus, the general rule of subparagraph 3(a) would not be applicable to the gain from the alienation of shares in the financial institution acquired after the entry into force of the Convention where the resident of the other Contracting State had acquired shares in the financial institution before the entry into force of the Convention.

Paragraph 4

Paragraph 4 deals with the taxation of certain gains from the alienation of property, other than real property, forming part of the business property of a permanent establishment that an enterprise of a Contracting State has in the other Contracting State. This also includes gains from the alienation of such a permanent establishment (alone or with the whole enterprise). Paragraph 3 preserves the non-exclusive right of the Contracting State in which the permanent establishment is located to tax such gains.

A resident of Japan that is a partner in a partnership doing business in the United States generally will have a permanent establishment in the United States as a result of the activities of the partnership, assuming that the activities of the partnership rise to the level of a permanent establishment. Rev. Rul. 91-32, 1991-1 C.B. 107. Further, under paragraph 3, the United States generally may tax a partner's distributive share of income realized by a partnership on the disposition of personal (movable) property forming part of the business property of the partnership in the United States.

Paragraph 5

This paragraph limits the taxing jurisdiction of the Contracting State of source with respect to gains from the alienation of ships or aircraft operated in international traffic by the enterprise alienating the ship or aircraft and from property (other than real property) pertaining to the operation or use of such ships, aircraft, or containers.

Under paragraph 5, such income is taxable only in the Contracting State in which the alienator is resident. Notwithstanding paragraph 4, the rules of this paragraph apply even if the income is attributable to a permanent establishment maintained by the enterprise in the other Contracting State. This result is consistent with the allocation of taxing rights under paragraph 1 of Article 8 (Shipping and Air Transport).

Paragraph 6

This paragraph limits the taxing jurisdiction of the Contracting State of source with respect to gains from the alienation of containers, except where such containers were used solely within that Contracting State.

Under paragraph 6, such income is taxable only in the Contracting State in which the alienator is resident. Notwithstanding paragraph 4, the rules of this paragraph apply even if the income is attributable to a permanent establishment maintained by the enterprise in the other Contracting State. This result is consistent with the allocation of taxing rights under paragraph 4 of Article 8 (Shipping and Air Transport).

Paragraph 7

Paragraph 7 grants to the Contracting State of residence of the alienator the exclusive right to tax gains from the alienation of property other than property referred to in the preceding paragraphs. For example, gain derived from shares (other than shares described in paragraphs 2, 3 or 4), debt instruments and various financial instruments, may be taxed only in the Contracting State of residence, to the extent such income is not otherwise characterized as income taxable under another article (*e.g.*, Article 10 (Dividends) or Article 11 (Interest)). Similarly, gain derived from the alienation of tangible personal property, other than tangible personal property described in paragraph 4, may be taxed only in the Contracting State of residence of the alienator. Sales by a resident of a Contracting State of real property located in a third state are not taxable in the other Contracting State, even if the sale is attributable to a permanent establishment located in the other Contracting State.

Relation to Other Articles

Notwithstanding the foregoing limitations on taxation of certain gains by the Contracting State of source, the saving clause of subparagraph 4(a) of Article 1 (General Scope) permits the United States to tax its citizens and residents as if the Convention had not come into effect. Thus, any limitation in this Article on the right of the United States to tax gains does not apply to gains of a U.S. citizen or resident.

The benefits of this Article are also subject to the provisions of Article 22 (Limitation on Benefits). Thus, only a resident of a Contracting State that satisfies one of the conditions in Article 22 is entitled to the benefits of this Article.

Article 14 (Income from Employment)

Article 14 apportions taxing jurisdiction over remuneration derived by a resident of a Contracting State as an employee between the States of source and residence.

Paragraph 1

The general rule of Article 14 is contained in paragraph 1. Remuneration derived by a resident of a Contracting State as an employee may be taxed by the Contracting State of residence, and the remuneration also may be taxed by the other Contracting State to the extent derived from employment exercised (*i.e.*, services performed) in that other Contracting State. Paragraph 1 also provides that the more specific rules of Articles 15 (Directors' Fees), 17 (Pensions, Social Security, Annuities, and Support Payments), and 18 (Government Service) apply in the case of employment income described in one of those articles. Thus, even though the Contracting State of source has a right to tax employment income under Article 14, it may not have the right to tax that income under the Convention if the income is described, for example, in Article 17 (Pensions, Social Security, Annuities, and Support Payments) and is not taxable in the Contracting State of source under the provisions of that article.

The Convention, like the OECD Model, refers to "salaries, wages and other similar remuneration," while the U.S. Model refers to "salaries, wages and other remuneration." The U.S. Model language was intended to make clear that Article 14 applies to any form of compensation, including payments in kind, regardless of whether the remuneration is "similar" to salaries or wages. The recent addition of paragraph 2.1 to the Commentary to Article 15 of the OECD Model, which confirms that payments in kind are covered by the Article, ensures that the language of the Convention and of the OECD Model reaches the same result as the language of the U.S. Model.

Consistent with section 864(c)(6) of the Code, Article 14 also applies regardless of the timing of actual payment for services. Thus, a bonus paid to a resident of a Contracting State with respect to services performed in the other Contracting State with respect to a particular taxable year would be subject to Article 14 for that year even if it was paid after the close of the year. Similarly, an annuity received for services performed in a taxable year would be subject to Article 14 despite the fact that it was paid in subsequent years. In either case, whether such payments were taxable in the Contracting State where the employment was exercised would depend on whether the tests of paragraph 2 were satisfied. Consequently, a person who receives the right to a future payment in consideration for services rendered in a Contracting State would be taxable in that State even if the payment is received at a time when the recipient is a resident of the other Contracting State.

Paragraph 10 of the Protocol contains special rules regarding employee stock options. Subparagraph (a) clarifies that any benefits enjoyed by employees under stock option plans relating to the period between grant and exercise of an option are regarded as "other similar remuneration" subject to Article 14.

Subparagraph (b) of paragraph 10 of the Protocol provides a specific rule for allocation of taxing rights where: (1) an employee has been granted a stock option in the course of employment in one of the Contracting States, (2) he has exercised that employment in both Contracting States during the period between grant and exercise of the option, (3) he remains in that employment at the date of the exercise, and (4), under the domestic law of the Contracting States, he would be taxable by both Contracting States in respect of the option gain. In this situation, each Contracting State may tax as Contracting State of source only that proportion of the option gain which relates to the period or periods between the grant and the exercise of the option during which the individual has exercised the employment in that Contracting State. The proportion attributable to a Contracting State is determined by multiplying the gain by a fraction, the numerator of which is the number of days during which the employee exercised his employment in that Contracting State and the denominator of which will be the total number of days between grant and exercise of the option. This allocation of taxing rights is provided in order to avoid double taxation.

Subparagraph (b) of paragraph 10 of the Protocol also provides that the competent authorities of the Contracting States, with the aim of ensuring that no unrelieved double taxation arises, will endeavor to resolve by mutual agreement any difficulties or doubts arising as to the interpretation or application of Article 14 and Article 23 (Relief from Double Taxation) in relation to employee stock option plans.

The rules of paragraph 10 of the Protocol are elaborated upon in an Understanding of the Negotiators, dated November 6, 2003, and attached to this Technical Explanation. The Understanding recognizes that the rules of the Convention, in particular the rule included in paragraph 10 of the Protocol, that allocate taxing jurisdiction between the Contracting States may not be enough to avoid double taxation in all cases involving employee stock option plans. The purpose of the Understanding is to establish a framework by which double taxation can be avoided to the maximum extent possible as provided for in subparagraph (b) of paragraph 10. The Understanding provides that in cases where the domestic law foreign tax credit provisions and the allocation rules of the Convention do not operate to completely alleviate double taxation, the competent authorities of Japan and the United States will, through a mutual agreement procedure, provide measures for the elimination of double taxation. Such measures may include the allowance of a foreign tax credit for taxes paid to the source country at the time of exercise or sale that are imposed in accordance with Article 14 and paragraph 10 of the Protocol. The limitations in the domestic law foreign tax credit provisions of Japan and the United States, such as limitations related to carryforward or carryback periods and limitations related to differences in the characterization of items of income or gain, will not prevent the alleviation of double taxation by the competent authorities in these cases. The Understanding further provides that in cases relating to stock options that raise other double taxation issues, the competent authorities will explore ways to reach appropriate agreement through the mutual agreement procedure on a case-by-case basis with the aim of ensuring no unrelieved double taxation.

Paragraph 2

Paragraph 2 sets forth an exception to the general rule in paragraph 1 that employment income may be taxed in the Contracting State where the employment is exercised. Under paragraph 2, the Contracting State where the employment is exercised may not tax the income from the employment if three conditions are satisfied: (1) the individual is present in the other Contracting State for a period or periods not exceeding 183 days in any 12-month period that begins or ends during the relevant (*i.e.*, the year in which the services are performed) calendar year; (2) the remuneration is paid by, or on behalf of, an employer who is not a resident of that other Contracting State; and (3) the remuneration is not borne by a permanent establishment that the employer has in that other Contracting State. In order for the remuneration to be exempt from tax in the source State, all three conditions must be satisfied. This exception is identical to that set forth in the U.S. and OECD Models.

The 183-day period is to be measured using the "days of physical presence" method. Under this method, the days that are counted include any day in which a part of the day is spent in the host country. *See* Rev. Rul. 56-24, 1956-1 C.B. 851. Thus, days that are counted include the days of arrival and departure; weekends and holidays on which the employee does not work but is present within the country; vacation days spent in the country before, during or after the employment period, unless the individual's presence before or after the employment can be shown to be independent of his presence there for employment purposes; and time during periods of sickness, training periods, strikes, etc., when the individual is present but not working. If illness prevented the individual from leaving the country in sufficient time to qualify for the benefit, those days will not count. Also, any part of a day spent in the host country while in transit between two points outside the host country is not counted. These rules are consistent with the description of the 183-day period in paragraph 5 of the Commentary to Article 15 in the OECD Model.

The second and third conditions are intended to ensure that a Contracting State will not be required to allow a deduction to the payer for compensation paid and at the same time to exempt the employee on the amount received. Accordingly, if a foreign person pays the salary of an employee who is employed in the host Contracting State, but a host Contracting State company or permanent establishment reimburses the payer with a payment that can be identified as a reimbursement, neither the second nor third conditions , as the case may be, will be considered to have been fulfilled.

The reference to remuneration "borne by" a permanent establishment is understood to encompass all expenses that economically are incurred and not merely expenses that are currently deductible for tax purposes. Accordingly, the expenses referred to include expenses that are capitalizable as well as those that are currently deductible. Further, salaries paid by residents that are exempt from income taxation may be considered to be borne by a permanent establishment notwithstanding the fact that the expenses will be neither deductible nor capitalizable since the payer is exempt from tax.

Paragraph 3 contains a special rule applicable to remuneration for services performed by an individual resident of one Contracting State as an employee aboard a ship or aircraft operated in international traffic. Under this paragraph, the employment income of such persons may be taxed in the Contracting State of residence of the enterprise operating the ship or aircraft. This is not an exclusive taxing right. The Contracting State of residence of the employee may also tax the remuneration. This provision is based on the OECD Model. U.S. internal law does not impose tax on non-U.S. source income of a person who is neither a U.S. citizen nor a U.S. resident, even if that person is an employee of a U.S. resident enterprise. Thus, under U.S. internal law the United States will not tax the salary of a resident of Japan who is employed by a U.S. carrier and who is not a U.S. citizen, except as provided in this Article.

Relation to other Articles

Notwithstanding the foregoing limitations on taxation of certain income by the Contracting State of source, the saving clause of subparagraph 4(a) of Article 1 (General Scope) permits the United States to tax its citizens and residents as if the Convention had not come into effect. Thus, any limitation in this Article on the right of the United States to tax income from employment does not apply to income of a U.S. citizen or resident.

Article 15 (Directors' Fees)

This Article provides that directors' fees and other similar payments derived by a resident of a Contracting State for services performed in his capacity as a director of the company which is a resident of the other Contracting State may be taxed in such other Contracting State. This rule is an exception to the more general rules of Articles 7 (Business Profits) and 14 (Income from Employment). Thus, a resident of one Contracting State who is a director of a company that is a resident of the other Contracting State is subject to tax in that other Contracting State in respect of his directors' fees regardless of where the services are performed. In determining whether a director's fee is subject to tax in the country of residence of the company, whether the fee is attributable to a permanent establishment is not relevant.

The provision in the Convention is identical to the analogous provision in the OECD Model. The U.S. Model reaches a different result, providing that the Contracting State of residence of the company may tax nonresident directors with no time or dollar threshold, but only with respect to remuneration for services performed in that Contracting State.

The Convention refers to "similar payments," while the U.S. Model refers to "other compensation." The U.S. Model language was intended to make clear that Article 15 applies to any form of compensation, including payments in kind, regardless of whether the remuneration is "similar" to directors' fees. The recent addition of paragraph 1.1 to the Commentary to Article 16 of the OECD Model, which confirms that payments in kind are covered by the Article, ensures that the language of the Convention and of the OECD Model reaches the same result as the language of the U.S. Model.

This Article does not grant an exclusive taxing right, nor does it limit the effect of the saving clause of subparagraph 4(a) of Article 1. Thus, if a U.S. citizen is a director of a Japanese corporation, the United States may tax his full remuneration, subject, of course, to any foreign tax credit that may be available.

Article 16 (Artistes and Sportsmen)

This Article deals with the taxation in a Contracting State of entertainers and sportsmen resident in the other Contracting State from the performance of their services as such. The Article applies both to the income of an entertainer or sportsman who performs services on his own behalf and one who performs services on behalf of another person, either as an employee of that person, or pursuant to any other arrangement. The rules of this Article take precedence, in some circumstances, over those of Articles 7 (Business Profits) and 14 (Income from Employment).

This Article applies only with respect to the income of entertainers and sportsmen. Others involved in a performance or athletic event, such as producers, directors, technicians, managers, coaches, etc., remain subject to the provisions of Articles 7 and 14. In addition, except as provided in paragraph 2 of Article 16, income earned by persons that are not individuals is not covered by Article 16.

Paragraph 1

Paragraph 1 describes the circumstances in which a Contracting State may tax the performance income of an entertainer or sportsman who is a resident of the other Contracting State. Under the paragraph, income derived by an individual resident of a Contracting State from activities as an entertainer or sportsman exercised in the other Contracting State may be taxed in that other Contracting State if the amount of the gross receipts derived by the performer exceeds $10,000 (or its equivalent in Japanese yen) for the taxable year. Gross receipts include expenses reimbursed to the individual or borne on his behalf. If the gross receipts exceed $10,000, the full amount, not just the excess, may be taxed in the Contracting State of performance.

The OECD Model provides for taxation by the country of performance of the remuneration of entertainers or sportsmen with no dollar or time threshold. This Convention introduces the dollar threshold test to distinguish between two groups of entertainers and athletes. The first group includes entertainers and athletes who are paid relatively large sums of money but are present in the country of performance for relatively short periods and because of that would be exempt from host country tax under the standard personal services income rules of Article 14. The second group includes entertainers and athletes who earn relatively modest amounts and therefore should be subject to the same rules of Article 14 that are applicable to those who earn other types of personal service income. The United States has entered a reservation to the OECD Model on the failure to provide such differentiation through a dollar threshold.

Tax may be imposed under paragraph 1 even if the performer would have been exempt from tax under Article 7 (Business Profits) or 14 (Income from Employment). On the other hand, if the performer would be exempt from host-country tax under Article 16, but would be taxable under either Article 7 or 14, tax may be imposed under either of those Articles. Thus, for example, if a performer derives remuneration from his activities in an independent capacity, and the performer does not have a permanent establishment in the host Contracting State, he may be taxed by the host Contracting State in accordance with Article 16 if his remuneration exceeds $10,000 annually, despite the fact that he generally would be exempt from host Contracting State taxation under Article 7. However, a performer who receives less than the $10,000 threshold amount and therefore is not taxable under Article 16, nevertheless may be subject to tax in the host country under Article 7 or 14 if the tests for host-country taxability under the relevant Article are met. For example, if an entertainer who is an independent contractor earns $7,000 of income in a Contracting State for the calendar year, but the income is attributable to his permanent establishment in the Contracting State of performance, that Contracting State may tax his income under Article 7.

Since it frequently is not possible to know until year-end whether the income an entertainer or sportsman derives from performances in a Contracting State will exceed $10,000, nothing in the Convention precludes that Contracting State from withholding tax during the year and refunding it after the close of the year if the taxability threshold has not been met.

As explained in paragraph 9 of the Commentary to Article 17 of the OECD Model, Article 16 of the Convention applies to all income connected with a performance by the entertainer, such as appearance fees, award or prize money, and a share of the gate receipts. Income derived from a Contracting State by a performer who is a resident of the other Contracting State from other than actual performance, such as royalties from record sales and payments for product endorsements, is not covered by this Article, but by other articles of the Convention, such as Article 12 (Royalties) or Article 7 (Business Profits). For example, if an entertainer receives royalty income from the sale of live recordings, the royalty income would be exempt from source state tax under Article 12, even if the performance was conducted in the source country, although the entertainer could be taxed in the source country with respect to income from the performance itself under Article 16 if the dollar threshold is exceeded.

In determining whether income falls under Article 16 or another article, the controlling factor will be whether the income in question is predominantly attributable to the performance itself or to other activities or property rights. For instance, a fee paid to a performer for endorsement of a performance in which the performer will participate would be considered to be so closely associated with the performance itself that it normally would fall within Article 16. Similarly, a sponsorship fee paid by a business in return for the right to attach its name to the performance would be so closely associated with the performance that it would fall under Article 16 as well. As indicated in paragraph 9 of the Commentary to Article 17 of the OECD Model, however, a cancellation fee would not be considered to fall within Article 16 but would be dealt with under Article 7 (Business Profits) or 14 (Income from Employment).

As indicated in paragraph 4 of the Commentary to Article 17 of the OECD Model, where an individual fulfills a dual role as performer and non-performer (such as a player-coach or an actor-director), but his role in one of the two capacities is negligible, the predominant character of the individual's activities should control the characterization of those activities. In other cases there should be an apportionment between the performance-related compensation and other compensation.

Consistent with Article 14 (Income from Employment), Article 16 also applies regardless of the timing of actual payment for services. Thus, a bonus paid to a resident of a Contracting State with respect to a performance in the other Contracting State during a particular taxable year would be subject to Article 16 for that year even if it was paid after the close of the year.

Paragraph 2

Paragraph 2 is intended to address the potential for circumvention of the rule in paragraph 1 when a performer's income does not accrue directly to the performer himself, but to another person. Foreign performers frequently perform in the United States as employees of, or under contract with, a company or other person.

The relationship may truly be one of employee and employer, with no circumvention of paragraph 1 either intended or realized. On the other hand, the "employer" may, for example, be a company established and owned by the performer, which is merely acting as the nominal income recipient in respect of the remuneration for the performance (a "star company"). The performer may act as an "employee," receive a modest salary, and arrange to receive the remainder of the income from his performance from the company in another form or at a later time. In such case, absent the provisions of paragraph 2, the income arguably could escape host-country tax because the company earns business profits but has no permanent establishment in that country. The performer may largely or entirely escape host-country tax by receiving only a small salary, perhaps small enough to place him below the dollar threshold in paragraph 1. The performer might arrange to receive further payments in a later year, when he is not subject to host-country tax, perhaps as dividends or liquidating distributions.

Paragraph 2 seeks to prevent this type of abuse while at the same time protecting the taxpayers' rights to the benefits of the Convention when there is a legitimate employee-employer relationship between the performer and the person providing his services. Under paragraph 2, when the income accrues to a person other than the performer, the income may be taxed in the Contracting State where the performer's services are exercised, without regard to the provisions of the Convention concerning business profits (Article 7) or income from employment (Article 14), unless the contract pursuant to which the personal activities are performed allows the person other than the performer to designate the individual who is to perform the personal activities. This rule is based on the U.S. domestic law provision characterizing income from certain personal service contracts as foreign personal holding company income in the context of the foreign personal holding company provisions. See Code sections 552 and 553. The premise of this rule is that, in a case where a performer is using another person in an attempt to circumvent the provisions of paragraph 1, the recipient of the services of the performer would contract with a person other than that performer (*i.e.*, a company employing the performer) only if the recipient of the services were certain that the performer himself would perform the services. If instead the person is allowed to designate the individual who is to perform the services, then likely the person is a service company not formed to circumvent the provisions of paragraph 1. The following example illustrates the operation of this rule.

Example. Company O, a resident of Japan, is engaged in the business of operating an orchestra. Company O enters into a contract with Company A pursuant to which Company O agrees to carry out two performances in the United States in consideration of which Company A will pay Company O $200,000. The contract designates two individuals, a conductor and a flutist, that must perform as part of the orchestra, and allows Company O to designate the other members of the orchestra. Because the contract does not give Company O any discretion to determine whether the conductor or the flutist perform personal services under the contract, the portion of the $200,000 which is attributable to the personal services of the conductor and the flutist may be taxed by the United States pursuant to paragraph 2. The remaining portion of the $200,000, which is attributable to the personal services of performers that Company O may designate, is not subject to tax by the United States pursuant to paragraph 2.

In cases where paragraph 2 is applicable, the income of the "employer" may be subject to tax in the host Contracting State even if it has no permanent establishment in the host country. Taxation under paragraph 2 is on the person providing the services of the performer. This paragraph does not affect the rules of paragraph 1, which apply to the performer himself. The income taxable by virtue of paragraph 2 is reduced to the extent of salary payments to the performer, which fall under paragraph 1.

For purposes of paragraph 2, income is deemed to accrue to another person (*i.e.*, the person providing the services of the performer) if that other person has control over, or the right to receive, gross income in respect of the services of the performer.

Since pursuant to Article 1 (General Scope) the Convention only applies to persons who are residents of one of the Contracting States, income of the star company would not be eligible for benefits of the Convention if the company is not a resident of one of the Contracting States.

Paragraph 2 differs from the analogous provision in the U.S. Model, paragraph 2 of Article 17 of the U.S. Model, although each is directed at mitigating the circumvention of paragraph 1 through the formation of an entity. Paragraph 2 of Article 17 of the U.S. Model looks to whether the performer participates in the profits of the company in any manner rather than whether the company has the ability to designate the individual to perform the services. Both Paragraph 2 of the Convention and the analogous provision in the U.S. Model are significantly narrower in scope than the analogous provision of the OECD Model, with respect to which the United States has entered a reservation.

Relationship to other Articles

This Article is subject to the provisions of the saving clause of subparagraph 4(a) of Article 1 (General Scope). Thus, if an entertainer or a sportsman who is resident in Japan is a citizen of the United States, the United States may tax all of his income from performances in the United States without regard to the provisions of this Article, subject, however, to the special foreign tax credit provisions of paragraph 3 of Article 23 (Relief from Double Taxation). In addition, benefits of this Article are subject to the provisions of Article 22 (Limitation on Benefits).

Article 17 (Pensions, Social Security, Annuities, and Support Payments)

This article deals with the taxation of private (*i.e.*, non-government service) pensions and annuities, social security benefits, and support payments.

Paragraph 1

Paragraph 1 provides, as a general rule, that the Contracting State of residence of the beneficial owner has the exclusive right to tax pensions and other similar remuneration. The phrase "pensions and other similar remuneration" includes both periodic and lump-sum payments.

The phrase "pension and other similar remuneration" is intended to encompass payments made by a pension fund, as defined in subparagraph 1(m) of Article 3 (General Definitions), or any other payment made by private retirement plans and arrangements in consideration of past employment.

Pensions in respect of government service (other than social security payments, as discussed below) generally are not covered by this paragraph, but rather are covered by paragraph 2 of Article 18 (Government Service). Thus, Article 18 covers section 457, 401(a) and 403(b) plans established for government employees. If a pension in respect of government service is not covered by Article 18 solely because the service is not "in the discharge of functions of a governmental nature," the pension is covered by this Article.

Paragraph 1 also provides for exclusive residence-country taxation of social security benefits. Like the prior Convention, but unlike the U.S. Model, the Convention provides that social security payments made by one of the Contracting States to a resident of the other Contracting State will be taxable only in the other Contracting State. This provision applies to social security beneficiaries, whether they have contributed to the system as private-sector or government employees. The provision is intended to include United States Tier 1 Railroad Retirement benefits.

Paragraph 2

Under paragraph 2, any annuities derived and beneficially owned by an individual who is a resident of a Contracting State is taxable only in that Contracting State. The term "annuities" means a stated sum paid periodically at stated times during the life of the individual, or during a specified or ascertainable period of time, under an obligation to make the payments in return for adequate and full consideration (other than in return for services rendered). The term "annuities" does not include any pensions or similar remuneration that is described in paragraph 1. Annuities received in consideration for services rendered would be treated as deferred compensation and generally taxable in accordance with Article 7 (Business Profits) or Article 14 (Income from Employment), not Article 17.

Paragraph 3

Paragraph 3 generally covers periodic payments made pursuant to a written separation agreement or a decree of divorce, separate maintenance, or compulsory support, including child support payments. Paragraph 3 exempts from tax in both Contracting States such payments made by a resident of one of the Contracting States to a resident of the other Contracting State, unless the payments are deductible in the payer's Contracting State of residence. Thus, support payments from a resident of a Contracting State to a resident of the other Contracting State are taxable in neither Contracting State if the support payments are not deductible to the payer. By contrast, deductible support payments made by a resident of a Contracting State to a resident of the other Contracting State are taxable, exclusively, in the recipient's State of residence. Although the structure of the Article is different, the results are the same as under the U.S Model provisions.

Relation to other Articles

Paragraphs 1 and 2 of Article 17 are subject to the saving clause of subparagraph 4(a) of Article 1 (General Scope). Thus, a U.S. citizen who is a resident of Japan and receives a pension, a social security payment, or an annuity payment will be subject to U.S. tax on the payment. However, paragraph 3 of Article 17 is not subject to the saving clause, by reason of the exception of paragraph 5 of Article 1. Accordingly, a U.S. citizen who is a resident of Japan will not be subject to U.S. tax on support payments made by a resident of the United States.

Article 18 (Government Service)

Paragraph 1

Subparagraphs (a) and (b) of paragraph 1 deal with the taxation of government compensation (other than a pension addressed in paragraph 2). Subparagraph (a) provides that remuneration paid from the public funds of one of the Contracting States or its political subdivisions or local authorities to any individual who is rendering services to that Contracting State, political subdivision or local authority is exempt from tax by the other Contracting State (the "host Contracting State"). Under subparagraph (b), such payments are, however, taxable exclusively in the other Contracting State (*i.e.*, the host Contracting State) if the services are rendered in that other Contracting State and the individual is a resident of that Contracting State who is either a national of that Contracting State or a person who did not become resident of that Contracting State solely for purposes of rendering the services.

This paragraph follows the OECD Model, but differs from the U.S. Model in applying only to government employees and not to independent contractors engaged by governments to perform services for them.

The remuneration described in paragraph 1 is subject to the provisions of this paragraph and not to those of Articles 14 (Income from Employment), 15 (Directors' Fees) or 16 (Artistes and Sportsmen). If, however, the recipient of the income is employed by a business conducted by a local government, paragraph 3 provides that those other Articles will apply.

Paragraph 2

Paragraph 2 deals with the taxation of pensions paid by, or out of funds to which contributions are made by, one of the Contracting States, or a political subdivision or a local authority thereof, to an individual in respect of services rendered to that Contracting State or subdivision or authority other than payments made by the United States under provisions of the social security or similar legislation. Subparagraph (a) provides that such pensions are taxable only in that Contracting State. Subparagraph (b) provides an exception under which such pensions are taxable only in the other Contracting State if the individual is a resident of, and a national of, that other Contracting State.

Pensions paid to retired civilian and military employees of a Government of either State are intended to be covered under paragraph 2. When payments made by the United States are under provisions of social security or similar legislation, however, those payments are covered by paragraph 1 of Article 17 (Pensions, Social Security, Annuities, and Support Payments). The phrase "similar legislation" is intended to refer to United States Tier 1 Railroad Retirement benefits. Paragraph 1 of Article 17 generally provides that social security benefits are taxable exclusively by the residence country

Paragraph 3

Paragraph 3 specifies that paragraphs 1 and 2 do not apply to remuneration and pensions paid for services performed in connection with a business carried on by a Contracting State or a political subdivision or local authority thereof. In such cases, the remuneration and pensions are subject instead to the provisions of Articles 14 (Income from Employment), 15 (Directors' Fees), 16 (Artistes and Sportsmen) and 17 (Pensions, Social Security, Annuities, and Support Payments). This provision conforms to the OECD Model.

Relation to other Articles

Article 18 is not subject to the saving clause of subparagraph 4(a) of Article 1 (General Scope), by reason of the exception in subparagraph 5 of Article 1, with respect to benefits conferred by Japan under Article 18 or benefits conferred by the United States under Article 18 to a resident of the United States who is neither a citizen of United States, nor a person who has been admitted for permanent residence there (*i.e.*, a "green card" holder). Article 18 is subject to the saving clause with respect to benefits conferred by the United States to citizens and permanent residents of the United States. Thus, for example, a resident of Japan who, in the course of rendering services to the government of Japan, becomes a resident of the United States (but not a permanent resident) would be entitled to the exemption from taxation by the Contracting State of source provided by paragraph 1. In addition, an individual who receives a pension paid by the Government of Japan in respect of services rendered to that Government is taxable on that pension only in Japan unless the individual is a U.S. citizen or acquires a U.S. green card.

Article 19 (Students)

Article 19 provides rules regarding the taxation of students and business apprentices. Persons who meet the tests of the article will be exempt from tax with respect to designated classes of income in the Contracting State they are visiting (the "host Contracting State"). Several conditions must be satisfied for an individual to be entitled to the benefits of this article.

First, the visitor must have been, either at the time of his arrival in the host Contracting State or immediately before, a resident of the other Contracting State.

Second, the primary purpose of the visit must be the education or training of the visitor. Thus, if the visitor comes principally to work in the host Contracting State but also is a part-time student, he is not entitled to the benefits of this article, even with respect to any payments he may receive from abroad for his maintenance or education, and regardless of whether or not he is in a degree program. A person who visits the host Contracting State to obtain business training and who also receives a salary from his employer for providing services would not be entitled to the benefits of this article with respect to the payments for services.

The host-country exemption in Article 19 applies only to payments arising outside the host Contracting State that are received by the student, apprentice or business trainee for the purpose of his maintenance, education or training. A payment will be considered to arise outside the host Contracting State if the payer is located outside the host Contracting State. Thus, if an employer from one of the Contracting States sends an employee to the other Contracting State for training, the payments the trainee receives from abroad from his employer for his maintenance or training while he is present in the host Contracting State will be exempt from tax in the host State. Where appropriate, substance prevails over form in determining the identity of the payer. Thus, for example, payments made directly or indirectly by a U.S. person with whom the visitor is training, but which have been routed through a source outside the United States (*e.g.*, a foreign bank account), are not treated as arising outside the United States for this purpose.

In the case of an apprentice or business trainee, the benefits of this article will extend only for a period of one year from the time that the visitor first arrives in the host Contracting State. If, however, an apprentice or trainee remains in the host Contracting State for a second year, thus losing the benefits of the article, he does not retroactively lose the benefits of the article for the first year.

Article 19 is not subject to the saving clause of subparagraph 4(a) of Article 1 (General Scope), by reason of the exception in subparagraph 5 of Article 1, with respect to benefits conferred by Japan under Article 19 or benefits conferred by the United States under Article 19 to a resident of the United States who is neither a citizen of United States, nor a person who has been admitted for permanent residence there (*i.e.*, a "green card" holder). Article 19 is subject to the saving clause with respect to benefits conferred by the United States to citizens and permanent residents of the United States. Accordingly, a U.S. citizen who is a resident of Japan and who visits the United States for the purpose of his education will not be exempt from U.S. tax on remittances from abroad that otherwise constitute U.S. taxable income. Under paragraph

5 of Article 1, however, a Japanese resident who is not a U.S. citizen, and who visits the United States for the purpose of his education and remains long enough to become a resident under U.S. law, but does not become a permanent resident (*i.e.*, does not acquire a green card), will be entitled to the benefits of Article 19.

Article 20 (Teachers)

Paragraph 1

Paragraph 1 provides rules regarding the taxation of teachers and researchers temporarily visiting one of the Contracting States. Persons who meet the tests of the article will be exempt from tax with respect to any remuneration for such teaching or research in the Contracting State they visiting (the "host Contracting State"). Several conditions must be satisfied for an individual to be entitled to the benefits of this article.

First, the visitor must be a resident, within the meaning of paragraph 1 of Article 4 (Residence), of the Contracting State other than the host Contracting State. The reference to paragraph 1 of Article 4 is intended to be a reference to the general rule for residence before the tie-breaker rules of paragraphs 2 and 3 of Article 4 are applied. Thus, an individual is a resident of a Contracting State for purposes of Article 20 and therefore may be entitled to benefits under Article 20 even though he is not a resident of that Contracting State for other purposes of the Convention under paragraphs 2 or 3 of Article 4. Individuals visiting one Contracting State (i.e., the host Contracting State) are treated as residents of the other Contracting State under paragraph 1 of Article 4 if they are liable to tax in that other Contracting State on the basis of the factors listed in paragraph 1 of Article 4. In the case of the United States, individuals who are United States citizens or aliens lawfully admitted for permanent residence in the United States are liable to tax in the United States on their world-wide income and therefore are residents of the United States under paragraph 1 of Article 4 even if they are not physically present in the United States. In the case of Japan, individuals who are employed by the Japanese Government are liable to tax in Japan on their world-wide income and therefore are residents of Japan under paragraph 1 of Article 4 even if they are not physically present Japan.

Second, the purpose of the visit must be to teach or conduct research at a university, college, school, or other educational institution in the host Contracting State. The phrase "university, college, school, or other educational institution" is understood not to require that the educational institution be accredited by an authority in the host Contracting State.

A teacher or researcher who satisfies these two conditions will be exempted from tax by the host Contracting State on any remuneration for such teaching or research for a period not exceeding two years from the date he first visits that Contracting State temporarily for the purpose of teaching or conducting research. Since this two year period is determined from the date he first visits the host Contracting State, periodic vacations outside the host Contracting State, or a brief return to the other Contracting State will not toll the running of the two year period. If the two-year period beginning from the date of his arrival is exceeded, the exemption will apply only for the first two years and only if the visit is temporary.

A person who meets the qualifications for this exemption may again claim its benefits if he first re-establishes his domicile in the other Contracting State. In such case, the person claiming these benefits on a subsequent occasion must first satisfy the competent authority of the host Contracting State that he had become a domiciliary of the other Contracting State for a substantial period of time (normally at least one year).

Paragraph 2

Pursuant to paragraph 3, this Article only applies to income from research undertaken in the public interest which is not primarily for the benefit of one or more specific persons. For example, research projects which are undertaken to discover or perfect product processes, designs, etc., which are expected to be commercially exploited by the researcher or his present (or former) employer do not qualify under this Article.

Relation to other Articles

Article 20 is not subject to the saving clause of subparagraph 4(a) of Article 1 (General Scope), by reason of the exception in subparagraph 5 of Article 1, with respect to benefits conferred by Japan or benefits conferred by the United States to a resident of the United States who is neither a citizen of United States, nor a person who has been admitted for permanent residence there (*i.e.*, a "green card" holder). Article 20 is subject to the saving clause with respect to benefits conferred by the United States to citizens and permanent residents of the United States. Accordingly, a U.S. citizen who is a resident of Japan and who visits the United States to teach at a university will not be exempt from U.S. tax on his salary. Under paragraph 5 of Article 1, however, a person who is not a U.S. citizen, and who visits the United States as a teacher and remains long enough to become a resident under U.S. law, but does not become a permanent resident (*i.e.*, does not acquire a green card), will be entitled to the benefits of Article 20.

Article 21 (Other Income)

Article 21 generally assigns exclusive taxing jurisdiction over income not dealt with in the other articles (Articles 6 through 20) of the Convention to the Contracting State of residence of the beneficial owner of the income. An item of income is "dealt with" in another article if it is the type of income described in the article and it has its source in a Contracting State. For example, all royalty income that arises in a Contracting State and that is beneficially owned by a resident of the other Contracting State is "dealt with" in Article 12 (Royalties).

Examples of items of income covered by Article 21 include income from gambling, punitive (but not compensatory) damages, covenants not to compete, and income from certain financial instruments to the extent derived by persons not engaged in the trade or business of dealing in such instruments (unless the transaction giving rise to the income is related to a trade or business, in which case it is dealt with under Article 7 (Business Profits)). The article also applies to items of income that are not dealt with in the other articles because of their source or some other characteristic. For example, Article 12 (Royalties) addresses only the taxation of royalties arising in a Contracting State. Royalties arising in a third State that is not attributable to a permanent establishment, therefore, is subject to Article 21.

Under paragraph 8 of the Protocol, fees in connection with a loan of securities, guarantee fees and commitment fees paid by a resident of a Contracting State and beneficially owned by a resident of the other Contracting State shall be taxable only in the Contracting State of residence unless such fees are attributable to a permanent establishment of the beneficial owner in the Contracting State of source. This rule is consistent with the rules applicable to income not dealt with in the taxing articles other than Article 21.

Distributions from partnerships are not generally dealt with under Article 21 because partnership distributions generally do not constitute income. Under the Code, partners include in income their distributive share of partnership income annually, and partnership distributions themselves generally do not give rise to income. This is also the case under U.S. law with respect to distributions from trusts. Under the Code, trust income and distributions have the character of the associated distributable net income and therefore would generally be covered by another article of the Convention. See Code section 641 et seq.

Paragraph 1

The general rule of Article 21 is contained in paragraph 1. Items of income not dealt with in other articles and beneficially owned by a resident of a Contracting State will be taxable only in the Contracting State of residence. This exclusive right of taxation applies whether or not the residence Contracting State exercises its right to tax the income covered by the Article.

The reference in this paragraph to "items of income beneficially owned by a resident of a Contracting State" rather than simply "items of income of a resident of a Contracting State," as in the OECD Model, is intended merely to make explicit the implicit understanding in other treaties that the exclusive residence taxation provided by paragraph 1 applies only when a resident of a Contracting State is the beneficial owner of the income. Thus, source taxation of income not dealt with in other articles of the Convention is not limited by paragraph 1 if it is nominally paid to a resident of the other Contracting State, but is beneficially owned by a resident of a third State. However, income received by a nominee on behalf of a resident of that other State would be entitled to benefits.

The term "beneficially owned" is not defined in the Convention, and is, therefore, defined as under the internal law of the country imposing tax (*i.e.*, the source country). The person who beneficially owns the income for purposes of Article 21 is the person to which the income is attributable for tax purposes under the laws of the source Contracting State.

Paragraph 2

This paragraph provides an exception to the general rule of paragraph 1 for income, other than income from real property, that is attributable to a permanent establishment maintained in a Contracting State by a resident of the other Contracting State. The taxation of such income is governed by the provisions of Article 7 (Business Profits). Therefore, income arising outside the

United States that is attributable to a permanent establishment maintained in the United States by a resident of Japan generally would be taxable by the United States under the provisions of Article 7. This would be true even if the income is sourced in a third State.

Paragraph 3

Paragraph 3 corresponds to rules dealing with interest and royalties in paragraph 8 of Article 11 (Interest) and paragraph 4 of Article 12 (Royalties). Paragraph 3 restricts the operation of Article 21 where, by reason of a special relationship between the payer and the beneficial owner or between both of them and some other person, the amount of other income paid exceeds the amount which would have been agreed upon by the parties had they stipulated at arm's length. This rule applies, for example, to payments pursuant to non-traditional financial instruments, such as equity swaps. Article 21 applies in such a case only to the arm's-length amount, and the excess part of the payment may be taxable in the Contracting State in which it arises at a rate not to exceed 5 percent. An explanation of this rule is provided in the explanation of paragraph 8 of Article 11 (Interest), above. Although paragraph 3 of Article 21 is not found in the U.S. or OECD Models, the Commentary to Article 21 of the OECD Model includes it as an optional provision of Article 21 of the OECD Model.

Paragraph 4

Paragraph 4 provides that a resident of a Contracting State shall not be considered the beneficial owner of other income in certain "back-to-back" arrangements. The benefits of Article 21 therefore are not available with respect to such other income. This rule is similar to rules dealing with interest, royalties, and other income in paragraph 11 of Article 10 (Dividends), paragraph 11 of Article 11 (Interest), and paragraph 5 of Article 12 (Royalties). These limited "anti-conduit" rules are discussed collectively in the explanation of paragraph 11 of Article 10 above.

Paragraph 4 in particular provides that a resident of a Contracting State shall not be considered the beneficial owner of other income in respect of a right or property if such other income would not have been paid unless the resident pays other income in respect of the same right or property to a person that is not entitled to the same or more favorable treaty benefits and that is not a resident of either Contracting State.

Relation to Other Articles

This Article is subject to the saving clause of subparagraph 4(a) of Article 1 (General Scope). Thus, the United States may tax the income of a resident of Japan that is not dealt with elsewhere in the Convention, if that resident is a citizen of the United States.

The benefits of this Article are also subject to the provisions of Article 22 (Limitation on Benefits). Thus, only a resident of a Contracting State that satisfies one of the conditions in Article 22 is entitled to the benefits of this Article.

Article 22 (Limitation on Benefits)

Purpose of Limitation on Benefits Provisions

The United States views an income tax treaty as a vehicle for providing treaty benefits to residents of the two Contracting States. The proper operation of a treaty requires that it apply to those that are *bona fide* residents of one of the Contracting States for the purpose of being granted treaty benefits. This principal has long been recognized. For example, the Commentaries to the OECD Model authorize a tax authority to deny treaty benefits, under substance-over-form principles, to a nominee in one Contracting State deriving income from the other on behalf of a third-country resident. In addition, although the text of the OECD Model does not contain express anti-abuse provisions, the Commentary to Article 1 contains an extensive discussion regarding the appropriateness of such provisions in tax treaties in order to limit the ability of third state residents to obtain treaty benefits. The United States holds strongly to the view that tax treaties should include provisions that specifically prevent misuse of treaties by residents of third countries. Consequently, all recent U.S. income tax treaties contain comprehensive Limitation on Benefits provisions.

A treaty that provides treaty benefits to *any* resident of a Contracting State permits "treaty shopping": the use, by residents of third states, of legal entities established in a Contracting State with a principal purpose to obtain the benefits of a tax treaty between the United States and the other Contracting State. Treaty shopping does not encompass every case in which a third state resident establishes an entity in a U.S. treaty partner, and that entity enjoys treaty benefits to which the third state resident would not itself be entitled. If the third country resident had substantial reasons for establishing the structure that were unrelated to obtaining treaty benefits, the use of the entity in the U.S. treaty partner would not fall within this concept of treaty shopping.

An anti-treaty shopping approach that required the tax authority to investigate the taxpayer's motives in establishing an entity in a particular country would be difficult to administer. In order to avoid the necessity of making such a subjective determination, Article 22 sets forth a series of objective tests. The assumption underlying each of these tests is that a taxpayer that satisfies the requirements of the test likely has a real business purpose for the structure it has adopted, or has a sufficiently strong nexus to the other Contracting State (*e.g.*, a resident individual) to warrant benefits even in the absence of a business connection, and that this business purpose or connection is sufficient to justify the conclusion that obtaining the benefits of the treaty is not a principal purpose of establishing or maintaining residence in that other Contracting State.

For instance, the assumption underlying the active trade or business test under paragraph 2 is that a third country resident that establishes a "substantial" operation in Japan and that derives income from a similar activity in the United States would not do so primarily to avail itself of the benefits of the Convention; it is presumed in such a case that the investor had a valid business purpose for investing in Japan, and that the link between that trade or business and the U.S. activity that generates the treaty-benefited income manifests a business purpose for placing the U.S. investments in the entity in Japan. It is considered unlikely that the investor would incur the expense of establishing a substantial trade or business in Japan simply to obtain the benefits of the Convention. A similar rationale underlies other tests in Article 22.

While these tests provide useful surrogates for identifying actual intent, these mechanical tests cannot account for every case in which the taxpayer was not treaty shopping. Accordingly, Article 22 also includes a provision (paragraph 4) authorizing the competent authority of a Contracting State to grant benefits in situations where none of the other tests of Article 22 is met. While an analysis under paragraph 4 may well differ from that under one of the other tests of Article 22, its objective is the same: to identify investors whose residence in the other Contracting State can be justified by factors other than a purpose to derive treaty benefits.

Article 22 and the anti-abuse provisions of domestic law complement each other, as Article 22 effectively determines whether an entity has a sufficient nexus to the Contracting State to be treated as a resident for treaty purposes, while domestic anti-abuse provisions (*e.g.,* business purpose, substance-over-form, step transaction or conduit principles) determine whether a particular transaction should be recast in accordance with its substance. Thus, internal law principles of the source Contracting State may be applied to identify the beneficial owner of an item of income, and Article 22 then will be applied to the beneficial owner to determine if that person is entitled to the benefits of the Convention with respect to such income.

Each of the substantive provisions of Article 22 states that benefits shall be granted only if the resident of a Contracting State satisfies any other specified conditions for claiming benefits. This means, for example, that a publicly-traded company that satisfies the conditions of subparagraph 1(c) will be eligible for the exemption from withholding tax on dividends at source only if it also owns more than 50 percent of the voting power of the paying company and satisfies the 12-month holding period requirement of subparagraph 3(a) of Article 10, and satisfies any other conditions specified in Article 10 or any other articles of the Convention.

Structure of the Article

Article 22 follows the form used in other recent U.S. income tax treaties. Paragraph 1 states the general rule that a resident of a Contracting State is entitled to benefits otherwise accorded to residents only to the extent that the resident satisfies the requirements of the Article and any other specified conditions for the obtaining of such benefits and then lists a series of attributes of a resident of a Contracting State, any one of which suffices to make such resident entitled to all the benefits of the Convention. Paragraph 2 sets forth the active trade or business test, under which a person not entitled to benefits under paragraph 1 may nonetheless be granted benefits with regard to certain types of income. Paragraph 4 provides that benefits may also be granted if the competent authority of the Contracting State from which the benefits are claimed determines that it is appropriate to grant benefits in that case. Paragraphs 3 and 5 set out rules of application and definitions of terms used specifically in this Article.

Paragraph 1

Paragraph 1 provides that, except as otherwise provided in Article 22, a resident of a Contracting State will be entitled to all the benefits of the Convention otherwise accorded to residents of a Contracting State only if the resident is described in one of the subparagraphs of that paragraph 1.

The benefits otherwise accorded to residents under the Convention include all limitations on source-based taxation under Articles 6 through 21, the treaty-based relief from double taxation provided by Article 23, and the protection afforded to residents of a Contracting State under Article 24. Some provisions do not require that a person be a resident in order to enjoy the benefits of those provisions. For example, Article 18 may apply to an employee of a Contracting State who is resident in neither State. Article 25 is not limited to residents of the Contracting States, and Article 28 applies to diplomatic agents or consular officials regardless of residence. Article 22 accordingly does not limit the availability of treaty benefits under these provisions.

Paragraph 1 has six subparagraphs, each of which describes a category of residents that are entitled to all benefits of the Convention. It is intended that the provisions of paragraph 1 will be self-executing. Claiming benefits under paragraph 1 does not require advance competent authority ruling or approval. The tax authorities may, of course, on review, determine that the taxpayer has improperly interpreted the paragraph and is not entitled to the benefits claimed.

Individuals -- Subparagraph 1(a)

Subparagraph (a) provides that individual residents of a Contracting State will be entitled to all benefits of the Convention. If such an individual receives income as a nominee on behalf of a third country resident, benefits may be denied under the respective articles of the Convention because in that case the beneficial owner of the income is not a resident of a Contracting State.

Governments and Central Banks -- Subparagraph 1(b)

Subparagraph (b) provides that the Contracting States, any political subdivision or local authority thereof, the Bank of Japan and the Federal Reserve Banks in the United States will be entitled to all benefits of the Convention.

Publicly-Traded Companies -- Subparagraph 1(c)

Subparagraph (c) applies to two categories of companies: publicly traded companies and subsidiaries of publicly traded companies. A company is entitled to all the benefits of the Convention under clause (i) of subparagraph (c) if the principal class of its shares, and any disproportionate class of shares, is listed on a recognized U.S. or Japanese stock exchange and is regularly traded on one or more recognized stock exchanges.

The term "principal class of shares" is not defined in the Convention and, accordingly, will be defined under the domestic laws of each Contracting State. In the United States, it means the common shares of the company representing the majority of the aggregate voting power and value of the company. If the company does not have a class of ordinary or common shares representing the majority of the aggregate voting power and value of the company, then the "principal class of shares" is that class or any combination of classes of shares that represents, in the aggregate, a majority of the voting power and value of the company.

The term "disproportionate class of shares" is defined in subparagraph (a) of paragraph 5. A company has a disproportionate class of shares if it has outstanding a class of shares which is subject to terms or other arrangements that entitle the holder to a larger portion of the company's income, profit, or gain in the other Contracting State than that to which the holder would be entitled in the absence of such terms or arrangements. Thus, for example, a company resident in Japan meets the test of subparagraph (a) of paragraph 5 if it has outstanding a class of "tracking stock" that pays dividends based upon a formula that approximates the company's return on its assets employed in the United States.

A company whose principal class of stock is publicly traded will nevertheless not qualify for benefits under subparagraph (c) of paragraph 1 if it has a disproportionate class of shares that is not publicly traded. The following example illustrates this result.

Example. JCo is a corporation resident in Japan. JCo has two classes of shares: Common and Preferred. The Common shares are listed and regularly traded on the Tokyo Stock Exchange. The Preferred shares have no voting rights and are entitled to receive dividends equal in amount to interest payments that JCo receives from unrelated borrowers in the United States. The Preferred shares are owned entirely by a single investor that is a resident of a country with which the United States does not have a tax treaty. The Common shares account for more than 50 percent of the value of JCo and for 100 percent of the voting power. Because the owner of the Preferred shares is entitled to receive payments corresponding to the U.S. source interest income earned by JCo, the Preferred shares are a disproportionate class of shares. Because the Preferred shares are not regularly traded on a recognized stock exchange, JCo will not qualify for benefits under subparagraph (c) of paragraph 1.

The term "recognized stock exchange" is defined in subparagraph (b) of paragraph 5 as (1) any stock exchange established under the terms of the Securities and Exchange Law (Law No. 25 of 1948) of Japan, including the Tokyo Stock Exchange; (2) the NASDAQ System owned by the National Association of Securities Dealers and any stock exchange registered with the Securities and Exchange Commission as a national securities exchange for purposes of the Securities Exchange Act of 1934; and (3) any other stock exchange agreed upon by the competent authorities of the Contracting States.

Under paragraph 11 of the Protocol, a class of shares will be considered to be "regularly traded" in a taxable year if the aggregate number of shares of that class traded on one or more recognized exchanges in the prior taxable year is at least six percent of the average number of shares outstanding in that class during that prior taxable year. Trading on one or more recognized stock exchanges may be aggregated for purposes of meeting the "regularly traded" standard of subparagraph (c). For example, a U.S. company could satisfy the definition of "regularly traded" by taking into account trading on both a recognized stock exchange located in the United States and a recognized stock exchange located in Japan. Authorized but unissued shares are not considered for purposes of subparagraph (c).

A company resident in a Contracting State is entitled to the benefits of the Convention under clause (ii) of subparagraph (c) of paragraph 1 if five or fewer direct and indirect owners of at least 50 percent of the aggregate vote and value of the company's shares are publicly traded companies described in clause (i). Thus, for example, a Japanese company, all the shares of which are owned by another Japanese company, would qualify for benefits under the Convention if the principal class of shares of the Japanese parent company were listed on the Tokyo Stock Exchange and regularly traded on the Tokyo Stock Exchange and the New York Stock Exchange. However, the Japanese company would not qualify for benefits under clause (ii) if the publicly traded parent company were a resident of Korea, not of the United States or Japan. Furthermore, if the Japanese parent indirectly owned the Japanese company through a chain of subsidiaries, each such subsidiary in the chain, as an intermediate owner, must be a resident of the United States or Japan that meets the requirements of clause (ii) in order for the Japanese company to meet the test in clause (ii).

With respect to withholding taxes, subparagraph (a) of paragraph 3 provides that the ownership requirements of clause (ii) of subparagraph (c) of paragraph 1 will be considered to be satisfied if they are met throughout a specified period. In general, the relevant period is the portion of the taxable year preceding the date on which the payment with respect to which benefits are claimed is made plus the entire preceding taxable year. In the case of dividend payments, the relevant end date of the period is the date on which entitlement to the dividend is determined rather than date on which the dividend is paid. (In the United States, this would be the "record date".) When the payment (or dividend record date) is the last day of the taxable year, the relevant period consists of only that taxable year, and no part of the preceding taxable year. The ownership requirements of clause (ii) also are satisfied if they are met throughout the taxable year with respect to which the benefits are claimed.

This ownership requirements of clause (ii) of subparagraph (c) of paragraph 1 differs from the requirements under clause (i) in that 50 percent of each class of the company's shares, not merely the class or classes accounting for more than 50 percent of the company's votes and value, must be held by publicly-traded companies described in clause 1(c)(i). Thus, the test under clause 1(c)(ii) considers the ownership of every class of shares outstanding, while the test under clause 1(c)(i) only considers those classes that account for a majority of the company's voting power and value as well as any disproportionate class of shares.

Tax Exempt Organizations -- Subparagraph 1(d)

Under subparagraph (d) of paragraph 1, a tax-exempt organization described in subparagraph (c) of paragraph 1 of Article 4 is entitled to all the benefits of the Convention, without regard to the residence of its beneficiaries or members. Entities qualifying under this subparagraph generally are those that are exempt from tax in their Contracting State of residence and that are organized and operated exclusively to fulfill religious, charitable, educational, scientific, artistic, cultural, or public purposes.

<u>Pension Funds – Subparagraph 1(e)</u>

A pension fund is entitled to all the benefits of the Convention if, as of the close of the end of the prior taxable year, more than 50 percent of the beneficiaries, members or participants of the organization are individuals resident in either Contracting State. For purposes of this provision, the term "beneficiaries" should be understood to refer to the persons receiving benefits from the organization.

<u>Ownership/Base Erosion -- Subparagraph 1(f)</u>

Subparagraph 1(f) provides an additional test that applies to any form of legal entity that is a resident of a Contracting State. The test provided in subparagraph (f), the so-called ownership and base erosion test, is a two-part test. Both prongs of the test must be satisfied for the resident to be entitled to benefits under subparagraph 1(f).

The ownership prong of the test, under clause (i), requires that 50 percent or more of each class of stock or other beneficial interests in the person be owned directly or indirectly by persons that themselves would be entitled to all the benefits of the Convention under specified other tests of paragraph 1 -- subparagraphs (a), (b), (d) or (e), or clause (i) of subparagraph (c). Paragraph (b) of paragraph 3 provides rules for determining whether the ownership prong of the test will be considered to be satisfied in the case of withholding taxes and other taxes.

With respect to withholding taxes, clause (i) of subparagraph (b) of paragraph 3 provides that the ownership prong of the test will be considered to be satisfied if the ownership requirements of clause (i) of subparagraph (f) of paragraph 1 are met throughout a specified period. In general, the relevant period is the portion of the taxable year preceding the date on which the payment with respect to which benefits are claimed is made plus the entire preceding taxable year. In the case of dividend payments, the relevant end date of the period is the date on which entitlement to the dividend is determined rather than when the dividend is paid. (In the United States, this would be the "record date".) When the payment (or dividend record date) is the last day of the taxable year, the relevant period consists of only that taxable year, and no part of the preceding taxable year. The ownership requirements of clause (i) also are satisfied if they are met throughout the taxable year with respect to which the benefits are claimed.

With respect to taxes other than withholding taxes, clause (ii) of subparagraph (b) of paragraph 3 provides that the ownership prong will be considered to be satisfied with respect to a taxable year only if the ownership requirement is met on at least half the days of the resident's taxable year in which the payment is made.

Trusts may be entitled to benefits under this provision if they are treated as residents under Article 4 and they otherwise satisfy the requirements of this subparagraph. For purposes of this subparagraph, the beneficial interests in a trust will be considered to be owned by its beneficiaries in proportion to each beneficiary's actuarial interest in the trust. The interest of a remainder beneficiary will be equal to 100 percent less the aggregate percentages held by income beneficiaries. A beneficiary's interest in a trust will not be considered to be owned by a person entitled to benefits under the other provisions of paragraph 1 if it is not possible to determine the beneficiary's actuarial interest. Consequently, if it is not possible to determine the actuarial interest of any beneficiaries in a trust, the ownership test under clause (i) cannot be satisfied, unless all possible beneficiaries are persons entitled to benefits under the other subparagraphs of paragraph 1.

The base erosion prong of clause (ii) of subparagraph (f) requires that less than 50 percent of a person's gross income for the taxable year is paid or accrued in that taxable year to a person or persons who are not residents of either Contracting State in the form of payments deductible for tax purposes in the payer's State of residence. Subparagraph (c) of paragraph 3 provides that, in the case of withholding taxes imposed by Japan on U.S. residents, this prong will be considered to be satisfied with respect to the taxable year in which a payment is made if the requirements were satisfied for each of the preceding three taxable years. The base erosion prong also is satisfied in the case of withholding taxes imposed by Japan and in all other cases if it is satisfied for the taxable year with respect to which the benefits are claimed.

Subparagraph (c) of paragraph 5 provides that the term "gross income" means total revenues derived by a resident of a Contracting State from its business, less the direct costs of obtaining such revenues. In the case of the United States, this definition corresponds to the definition of the term "gross income" in section 61 of the Code and the regulations thereunder.

Depreciation and amortization deductions, which do not represent payments or accruals to other persons, are disregarded for the purpose of determining gross income. Deductible payments do not include arm's length payments in the ordinary course of business for services or tangible property or with respect to financial obligations to banks that are residents of either Contracting State, or that have a permanent establishment in either Contracting State to which the payment is attributable. To the extent they are deductible from the taxable base, however, trust distributions are deductible payments.

Paragraph 2

Paragraph 2 sets forth a test under which a resident of a Contracting State that is not entitled to all the benefits of the Convention under paragraph 1 may receive treaty benefits with respect to certain items of income that are connected to an active trade or business conducted in its State of residence.

Subparagraph (a) sets forth the general rule that a resident of a Contracting State engaged in the active conduct of a trade or business in that Contracting State may obtain the benefits of the Convention with respect to an item of income derived in the other Contracting State. The item of income, however, must be derived in connection with or be incidental to that trade or business.

The term "trade or business" is not defined in the Convention. Pursuant to paragraph 2 of Article 3 (General Definitions), when determining whether a resident of Japan is entitled to the benefits of the Convention under paragraph 2 of this Article with respect to an item of income, profit, or gains derived from sources within the United States, the United States will interpret this term in accordance with the meaning that it has under the law of the United States. Accordingly, the U.S. competent authority will refer to the regulations issued under section 367(a) for the definition of the term "trade or business." In general, therefore, a trade or business will be considered to be a specific unified group of activities that constitute or could constitute an independent economic enterprise carried on for profit. Furthermore, a company generally will be considered to carry on a trade or business only if the officers and employees of the company conduct substantial managerial and operational activities.

The business of making or managing investments for the resident's own account will be considered to be a trade or business only when part of banking, insurance or securities activities conducted by a bank, an insurance company, or a registered securities dealer. Such activities conducted by a person other than a bank, insurance company or registered securities dealer will not be considered to be the conduct of an active trade or business, nor would they be considered to be the conduct of an active trade or business if conducted by a bank, insurance company or registered securities dealer but not as part of the company's banking, insurance or dealer business.

Because a headquarters operation is in the business of managing investments, a company that functions solely as a headquarters company will not be considered to be engaged in an active trade or business for purposes of subparagraph (a).

Income is derived in connection with a trade or business if the income-producing activity in the Contracting State of source is a line of business that "forms a part of" or is "complementary" to the trade or business conducted in the Contracting State of residence by the income recipient.

A business activity generally will be considered to form part of a business activity conducted in the Contracting State of source if the two activities involve the design, manufacture or sale of the same products or type of products, or the provision of similar services. The line of business in the Contracting State of residence may be upstream, downstream, or parallel to the activity conducted in the Contracting State of source. Thus, the line of business may provide inputs for a manufacturing process that occurs in the Contracting State of source, may sell the output of that manufacturing process, or simply may sell the same sorts of products that are being sold by the trade or business carried on in the Contracting State of source.

Example 1. USCo is a corporation resident in the United States. USCo is engaged in an active manufacturing business in the United States. USCo owns 100 percent of the shares of JCo, a company resident in Japan. JCo distributes USCo products in Japan. Because the business activities conducted by the two corporations involve the same products, JCo's distribution business is considered to form a part of USCo's manufacturing business.

Example 2. The facts are the same as in Example 1, except that USCo does not manufacture. Rather, USCo operates a large research and development facility in the United States that licenses intellectual property to affiliates worldwide, including JCo. JCo and other USCo affiliates then manufacture and market the USCo-designed products in their respective markets. Because the activities conducted by JCo and USCo involve the same product lines, these activities are considered to form a part of the same trade or business.

For two activities to be considered to be "complementary," the activities need not relate to the same types of products or services, but they should be part of the same overall industry and be related in the sense that the success or failure of one activity will tend to result in success or failure for the other. Where more than one trade or business is conducted in the Contracting State of source and only one of the trades or businesses forms a part of or is complementary to a trade or business conducted in the Contracting State of residence, it is necessary to identify the trade or business to which an item of income is attributable. Royalties generally will be considered to be derived in connection with the trade or business to which the underlying intangible property is attributable. Dividends will be deemed to be derived first out of earnings and profits of the treaty-benefited trade or business, and then out of other earnings and profits. Interest income may be allocated under any reasonable method consistently applied. A method that conforms to U.S. principles for expense allocation will be considered a reasonable method.

Example 3. Americair is a corporation resident in the United States that operates an international airline. JSub is a wholly-owned subsidiary of Americair resident in Japan. JSub operates a chain of hotels in Japan that are located near airports served by Americair flights. Americair frequently sells tour packages that include air travel to Japan and lodging at JSub hotels. Although both companies are engaged in the active conduct of a trade or business, the businesses of operating a chain of hotels and operating an airline are distinct trades or businesses. Therefore JSub's business does not form a part of Americair's business. However, JSub's business is considered to be complementary to Americair's business because they are part of the same overall industry (travel), and the links between their operations tend to make them interdependent.

Example 4. The facts are the same as in Example 3, except that JSub owns an office building in Japan instead of a hotel chain. No part of Americair's business is conducted through the office building. JSub's business is not considered to form a part of or to be complementary to Americair's business. They are engaged in distinct trades or businesses in separate industries, and there is no economic dependence between the two operations.

Example 5. USFlower is a company resident in the United States. USFlower produces and sells flowers in the United States and other countries. USFlower owns all the shares of JHolding, a corporation resident in Japan. JHolding is a holding company that is not engaged in a trade or business. JHolding owns all the shares of three corporations that are resident in Japan: JFlower, JLawn, and JFish. JFlower distributes USFlower flowers under the USFlower trademark in Japan. JLawn markets a line of lawn care products in Japan under the USFlower trademark. In addition to being sold under the same trademark, JLawn and JFlower products are sold in the same stores and sales of each company's products tend to generate increased sales of the other's products. JFish imports fish from the United States and distributes it to fish wholesalers in Japan. For purposes of paragraph 2, the business of JFlower forms a part of the business of USFlower, the business of JLawn is complementary to the business of USFlower, and the business of JFish is neither part of nor complementary to that of USFlower.

Finally, an item of income derived from the Contracting State of source is "incidental to" the trade or business carried on in the Contracting State of residence if production of the item facilitates the conduct of the trade or business in the Contracting State of residence. An example of incidental income is the temporary investment of working capital of a person in the Contracting State of residence in securities issued by persons in the Contracting State of source.

Subparagraph (b) of paragraph 2 states a further condition to the general rule in subparagraph (a) in cases where the trade or business generating the item of income in question is carried on either by the person deriving the income or by any associated enterprises. Subparagraph (b) states that the trade or business carried on in the Contracting State of residence, under these circumstances, must be substantial in relation to the activity in the Contracting State of source. This determination is made based upon all the facts and circumstances and takes into account the comparative sizes of the trades or businesses in each Contracting State (measured by reference to asset values, income and payroll expenses), the nature of the activities performed in each Contracting State, and the relative contributions made to that trade or business in each Contracting State.

The substantiality requirement is intended to prevent a narrow case of treaty-shopping abuses in which a company attempts to qualify for benefits by engaging in de minimis connected business activities in the treaty country in which it is resident (*i.e.*, activities that have little economic cost or effect with respect to the company business as a whole).

The application of the substantiality test only to income from related parties focuses only on potential abuse cases, and does not hamper certain other kinds of non-abusive activities, even though the income recipient resident in a Contracting State may be very small in relation to the entity generating income in the other Contracting State. For example, if a small U.S. research firm develops a process that it licenses to a very large, unrelated, Japanese electronics manufacturer, the size of the U.S. research firm would not have to be tested against the size of the Japanese manufacturer. Similarly, a small U.S. bank that makes a loan to a very large unrelated Japanese business would not have to pass a substantiality test under subparagraph (b) in order to receive treaty benefits.

Paragraph 12 of the Protocol provides special rules for determining whether a resident of a Contracting State is engaged in the active conduct of a trade or business within the meaning of subparagraph (a). Under that paragraph, the activities of a partnership are attributed to each of its partners. The paragraph also attributes to a person activities conducted by persons "connected" to such person. A person ("X") is connected to another person ("Y") if X possesses 50 percent or more of the beneficial interest in Y (or if Y possesses 50 percent or more of the beneficial interest in X). For this purpose, X is connected to a company if X owns shares representing 50 percent or more of the aggregate voting power and value of the company or 50 percent or more of the beneficial equity interest in the company. X also is connected to Y if a third person possesses 50 percent or more of the beneficial interest in both X and Y. For this purpose, if X or Y is a company, the threshold relationship with respect to such company or companies is 50 percent or more of the aggregate voting power and value or 50 percent or more of the beneficial equity interest.

Paragraph 3

Paragraph 3 includes rules regarding the application of the ownership tests under clause (ii) of subparagraph (c) of paragraph 1 and clause (i) of subparagraph (f) of paragraph 1 and the base erosion test under clause (ii) of subparagraph (f) or paragraph 1. These rules, which are discussed above in connection with the tests to which they relate, provide in particular in the case of withholding taxes that those tests will be considered to be satisfied if they are satisfied for specified periods ending on or before the date on which the income that may be entitled to treaty benefits is paid. Providing rules that allow withholding agents to determine with certainty whether these tests are met on the date of payment is particularly important in light of the obligations imposed on withholding agents by the Japanese withholding system. These rules ensure that withholding agents are able to withhold the appropriate amount of tax, if any, under the Convention at the time of the payment.

Paragraph 4

Paragraph 4 provides that a resident of one of the Contracting States that is neither described in paragraph 1 nor entitled to the benefits of the Convention with respect to an item of income under paragraph 2 of this article still may be granted benefits under the Convention at the discretion of the competent authority of the Contracting State from which benefits are claimed. In making determinations under paragraph 4, that competent authority will take into account as its guideline whether the establishment, acquisition, or maintenance of the person seeking benefits under the Convention, or the conduct of such person's operations, has or had as one of its principal purposes the obtaining of benefits under the Convention. Thus, persons that establish operations in one of the Contracting States with a principal purpose of obtaining the benefits of the Convention ordinarily will not be granted relief under paragraph 4.

The competent authority may determine to grant all benefits of the Convention, or it may determine to grant only certain benefits. For instance, it may determine to grant benefits only with respect to a particular item of income in a manner similar to paragraph 2. Further, the competent authority may set time limits on the duration of any relief granted.

For purposes of implementing paragraph 4, a taxpayer will be permitted to present its case to the relevant competent authority for an advance determination based on the facts. In these circumstances, it is also expected that if the competent authority determines that benefits are to be allowed, they will be allowed retroactively to the time of entry into force of the relevant treaty provision or the establishment of the structure in question, whichever is later.

Paragraph 5

Paragraph 5 defines several key terms for purposes of Article 22. Each of the defined terms is discussed above in connection with the subparagraphs of paragraph 1 in which it occurs.

Article 23 (Relief from Double Taxation)

This Article addresses the manner in which each Contracting State undertakes to relieve double taxation. The United States uses the foreign tax credit method under its internal law and by treaty.

Paragraph 1

Japan agrees, in paragraph 1, to allow to its residents a credit against Japanese tax for U.S. taxes. For this purpose, the U.S. taxes covered by subparagraph 1(b) and paragraph 2 of Article 2 (Taxes Covered) are U.S. taxes.

Under subparagraph (a) of paragraph 1 of Article 23, where a resident of Japan derives income from the United States which may be taxed in the United States in accordance with this Convention, the amount of U.S. tax payable in respect of that income is allowed as a credit against the Japanese tax imposed on that resident. The amount of credit, however, shall not exceed that part of the Japanese tax which is appropriate to that income.

Under subparagraph (b), in the case of a dividend paid by a company that is a resident of the United States to a company that is a resident of Japan and which owns not less than 10 percent of the voting shares issued by the company paying the dividend during the period of six months immediately before the day when the obligation to pay dividends is confirmed, the credit against Japanese tax takes into account the U.S. tax payable by the company paying the dividends in respect of its income.

The credits allowed under paragraph 1 are allowed subject to the provisions of the laws of Japan regarding the allowance as a credit against Japanese tax of tax payable in other countries.

The last sentence of paragraph 1 provides a re-sourcing rule for income covered by paragraph 1. This provision is intended to ensure that a Japanese resident can obtain a Japanese foreign tax credit for U.S. taxes paid when the Convention assigns to the United States primary taxing rights over an item of income. The last sentence of paragraph 1 provides that, if the Convention allows the United States to tax an item of income beneficially owned by a resident of Japan, that income will be deemed to arise from sources in the United States for Japanese foreign tax credit purposes. However, paragraph 3 of this article provides special rules where a resident of Japan is a U.S. citizen, a former U.S. citizen, or a former U.S. long-term resident and is subject to tax in the United States solely by reason of the provisions of paragraph 4 of Article 1 (General Scope).

Paragraph 2

The United States agrees, in paragraph 2, to allow to its residents a credit against U.S. tax for Japanese taxes. For this purpose, the U.S. taxes covered by subparagraph 1(b) and paragraph 2 of Article 2 (Taxes Covered) are U.S. taxes.

Subparagraph (a) of paragraph 2 provides for the allowance to U.S. citizens and residents a credit against U.S. tax for income taxes paid or accrued to Japan. Subparagraph (b) provides for a deemed-paid credit, consistent with section 902 of the Code, to a U.S. company in respect of dividends received from a company resident in Japan of which the U.S. company owns at least 10 percent of the voting stock. This credit is for the tax paid by the Japanese company on the profits out of which the dividends are considered paid.

For the purpose of paragraph 2, the Japanese taxes covered by subparagraph (a) of paragraph 1 of Article 2 (Taxes Covered) shall be considered Japanese taxes imposed on the beneficial owner of the income. This makes clear that Japanese withholding taxes described by subparagraph (a) of paragraph 1 of Article 2 with respect to income beneficially owned by a U.S. resident or citizen shall be creditable.

The credits allowed under paragraph 2 are allowed in accordance with the provisions and subject to the limitations of U.S. law, as that law may be amended over time, so long as the general principle of the Article, that is, the allowance of a credit, is retained. Thus, although the Convention provides for a foreign tax credit, the terms of the credit are determined by the provisions, at the time a credit is given, of the U.S. statutory foreign tax credit.

The U.S. credit under the Convention is subject to the various limitations of U.S. law (see Code sections 901-908). For example, the credit against U.S. tax generally is limited to the amount of U.S. tax due with respect to net foreign source income within the relevant foreign tax credit limitation category (see Code section 904(a) and (d)), and the dollar amount of the credit is determined in accordance with U.S. currency translation rules (see, *e.g.*, Code section 986). Similarly, U.S. law applies to determine carryover periods for excess credits and other inter-year adjustments. When the alternative minimum tax is due, the alternative minimum tax foreign tax credit generally is limited in accordance with U.S. law to 90 percent of alternative minimum tax liability.

The last sentence of paragraph 2 provides a re-sourcing rule for gross income covered by paragraph 2. This provision is intended to ensure that a U.S. resident can obtain a U.S. foreign tax credit for Japanese taxes paid when the Convention assigns to Japan primary taxing rights over an item of gross income. Although the U.S. Model does not contain a re-sourcing rule, the prior Convention does contain a similar rule, as do many other U.S. treaties.

The last sentence of paragraph 2 provides that, if the Convention allows Japan to tax an item of gross income (as defined under U.S. law) derived by a resident of the United States, the United States will treat that item of gross income as gross income from sources within Japan for U.S. foreign tax credit purposes. In the case of a U.S.-owned foreign corporation, however, section 904(g)(10) may apply for purposes of determining the U.S. foreign tax credit with respect to income subject to this re-sourcing rule. Section 904(g)(10) generally applies the foreign tax credit limitation separately to re-sourced income. Furthermore, the paragraph 2 re-sourcing rule applies to gross income, not net income. Accordingly, U.S. expense allocation and apportionment rules, see, *e.g.*, Treas. Reg. section 1.861-9, continue to apply to income resourced under paragraph 2.

Paragraph 3 provides special rules for the allowance of a foreign tax credit in both Contracting States in cases where the United States taxes, in accordance with paragraph 4 of Article 1, a resident of Japan who is a U.S. citizen, a former U.S. citizen, or a former long-term resident of the United States. Paragraph 4 of Article 1 includes the saving clause, pursuant to which the United States may tax U.S. citizens as if the Convention had not come into effect, and rules regarding the taxation in certain circumstances by the United States of former U.S. citizens and former U.S. long-term residents. Because U.S. citizens are subject to United States tax at statutory rates on their worldwide income, the U.S. tax on the U.S. source income of a U.S. citizen that is a resident of Japan may exceed the U.S. tax that may be imposed under the Convention on an item of U.S. source income derived by a resident of Japan who is not a U.S. citizen. Similarly, the U.S. tax on the U.S. source income of a resident of Japan that is a former U.S. citizen or a former U.S. long-term resident may exceed the U.S. tax that may be imposed under the Convention on an item of U.S. source income derived by a resident of Japan who is not a former U.S. citizen or a former U.S. long-term resident.

Paragraph 3 does not apply to the extent that the United State imposes tax on a U.S. citizen, former U.S. citizen, or former U.S. long-term resident in a manner that is consistent with the provisions of the Convention other than paragraph 4 of Article 1. For example, paragraph 3 of Article 14 (Income from Employment) allows a Contracting State to tax remuneration derived by an individual that is not a resident in respect of an employment exercised aboard a ship or aircraft operated in international traffic by an enterprise of that Contracting State. Under its domestic law, the United States generally could tax an individual in such a case only if that individual is a citizen. Because such taxation would be consistent with the provisions of the Convention other than other than paragraph 4 of Article 1, the special rules of paragraph 3 of Article 23 would not apply to such taxation.

Subparagraph 3(a) follows the U.S. Model by providing, with respect to items of income from sources within the United States, special foreign tax credit rules for Japan. These rules apply to items of U.S.-source income that would be either exempt from U.S. tax or subject to reduced rates of U.S. tax under the provisions of the Convention if they had been received by a Japanese resident who is not a U.S. citizen, a former U.S. citizen, or a former U.S. long-term resident. For purposes of computing the foreign tax credit allowed under paragraph 1, Japan will take into account only the U.S. tax that may be imposed under the Convention, without regard to the rules of paragraph 4 of Article 1 (General Scope) and thus will not include the tax imposed solely by reason of the provisions of the saving clause and rules regarding the taxation of former U.S. citizens and long-term residents of paragraph 4 of Article 1.

For example, if a U.S. citizen resident in Japan receives portfolio dividends from sources within the United States, the foreign tax credit granted by Japan would be limited to 10 percent of the dividend -- the U.S. tax that may be imposed under subparagraph (b) of paragraph 2 of Article 10 (Dividends) -- even though the shareholder is subject to U.S. net income tax because of his U.S. citizenship. With respect to royalty income, Japan would allow no foreign tax credit, because its residents are exempt from U.S. tax on these classes of income under the provisions of Article 12 (Royalties).

Subparagraph 3(b) eliminates the potential for double taxation that can arise because subparagraph (a) provides that Japan need not provide full relief for the U.S. tax imposed on residents of Japan who are U.S. citizens, former U.S. citizens, or former U.S. long-term residents. The subparagraph provides that the United States will credit the Japanese tax, after the application of subparagraph (a). It further provides that in allowing the credit, the United States will not reduce its tax below the amount that is taken into account in Japan in applying subparagraph (a).

Since the income described in paragraph (a) is U.S. source income, special rules are required to re-source some of the income to Japan in order for the United States to be able to credit the Japanese tax. This re-sourcing is provided for in subparagraph (c), which deems the items of income referred to in subparagraph (a) to be from foreign sources to the extent necessary to avoid double taxation under paragraph (b).

The following two examples illustrate the application of paragraph 3 in the case of a U.S.-source portfolio dividend received with respect to stock held for less than one year by a U.S. citizen who is a resident of Japan. In both examples, the U.S. rate of tax on residents of Japan, under subparagraph (b) of paragraph 2 of Article 10 (Dividends), is 10 percent. In both examples, the U.S. income tax rate on the U.S. citizen is 36 percent. In example 1, the Japanese income tax rate on the resident of Japan (the U.S. citizen) is 25 percent (below the U.S. rate), and in example 2, the Japanese rate on the resident of Japan is 40 percent (above the U.S. rate).

	Example 1	Example 2
Subparagraph (a)		
U.S. dividend declared	$100.00	$100.00
Notional U.S. withholding tax (Article 10(2)(b))	10.00	10.00
Japanese taxable income	100.00	100.00
Japanese tax before credit	25.00	40.00
Japanese foreign tax credit	10.00	10.00
Net post-credit Japanese tax	15.00	30.00
Subparagraphs (b) and (c)		
U.S. pre-tax income	$100.00	$100.00
U.S. pre-credit citizenship tax	36.00	36.00
Notional U.S. withholding tax	10.00	10.00
U.S. tax available for offset by foreign tax credit	26.00	26.00
Income re-sourced from U.S. to Japan (see below)	41.67	72.22
U.S. tax on re-sourced income	15.00	26.00
U.S. foreign tax credit for Japanese tax	15.00	26.00
Net post-credit U.S. tax	11.00	0.00
Total U.S. tax	21.00	10.00

In both examples, in the application of subparagraph (a), Japan credits a 10 percent U.S. tax against its residence tax on the U.S. citizen. In the first example, the net Japanese tax after the Japanese foreign tax credit is $15.00; in the second example, it is $30.00. In the application of subparagraphs (b) and (c), from the U.S. tax due before credit of $36.00, the United States subtracts the amount of the U.S. source tax of $10.00, against which no U.S. foreign tax credit is allowed. This subtraction ensures that the United States collects the tax that it is due under the Convention as the Contracting State of source.

In both examples, given the 36 percent U.S. tax rate, the maximum amount of U.S. tax against which credit for the Japanese tax may be claimed is $26 ($36 U.S. tax minus $10 U.S. withholding tax). Initially, all of the income in both examples was from sources within the United States. For a U.S. foreign tax credit to be allowed for the full amount of the Japanese tax, an appropriate amount of the income must be re-sourced to Japan under subparagraph (c).

The amount that must be re-sourced depends on the amount of Japanese tax for which the U.S. citizen is claiming a U.S. foreign tax credit. In example 1, the Japanese tax is $15. For this amount to be creditable against U.S. tax, $41.67 ($15 Japanese tax divided by 36 percent U.S. tax rate) must be re-sourced to Japan. When the Japanese tax is credited against the U.S. tax on this re-sourced income, there is a net U.S. tax of $11 due after credit ($26 U.S. tax minus $15 Japanese tax). Thus, in example 1, there is a total of $21 in U.S. tax ($10 U.S. withholding tax plus $11 residual U.S. tax).

In example 2, the Japanese tax is $30 but, because the United States subtracts the U.S. withholding tax of $10 from the total U.S. tax of $36, only $26 of U.S. taxes may be offset by Japanese taxes. Accordingly, the amount that must be re-sourced to Japan is limited to the amount necessary to ensure a U.S. foreign tax credit for $26 of Japanese tax, or $72.22 ($26 Japanese tax divided by 36 percent U.S. tax rate). When the Japanese tax is credited against the U.S. tax on this re-sourced income, there is no residual U.S. tax ($26 U.S. tax minus $26 Japanese tax). Thus, in example 2, there is a total of $10 in U.S. tax ($10 U.S. withholding tax plus $0 residual U.S. tax). Although the Japanese tax is $30 and the U.S. tax available for offset by the foreign tax credit is $26, there is no excess U.S. tax credit available for carryover.

Relationship to other Articles

By virtue of paragraph 5 of Article 1 (General Scope), Article 24 is not subject to the saving clause of paragraph 4 of Article 1. Thus, the United States will allow a credit to its citizens and residents in accordance with the Article, even if such credit were to provide a benefit not available under the Code (such as the re-sourcing provided by the last sentence of paragraph 2 and by subparagraph 3(c)).

Article 24 (Non-Discrimination)

This Article ensures that nationals of a Contracting State, in the case of paragraph 1, and residents of a Contracting State, in the case of paragraphs 2 through 4, will not be subject, directly or indirectly, to discriminatory taxation in the other Contracting State. For this purpose, non-discrimination means providing national treatment. Not all differences in tax treatment, either as between nationals of the two Contracting States, or between residents of the two Contracting States, are violations of this national treatment standard. Rather, the national treatment obligation of this Article applies only if the nationals or residents of the two Contracting States are comparably situated.

Each of the relevant paragraphs of the Article provides that two persons that are comparably situated must be treated similarly. Although the actual words differ from paragraph to paragraph (*e.g.*, paragraph 1 refers to two nationals "in the same circumstances," paragraph 2 refers to two enterprises "carrying on the same activities" and paragraph 4 refers to two enterprises that are "similar"), the common underlying premise is that if the difference in treatment is directly related to a tax-relevant difference in the situations of the domestic and foreign persons being compared, that difference is not to be treated as discriminatory (i.e., if one person is taxable in a Contracting State on worldwide income and the other is not, or tax may be collectible from one person at a later stage, but not from the other, distinctions in treatment would be justified under paragraph 1). Other examples of such factors that can lead to non-discriminatory differences in treatment are noted in the discussions of each paragraph.

The operative paragraphs of the Article also use different language to identify the kinds of differences in taxation treatment that will be considered discriminatory. For example, paragraphs 1 and 4 speak of "any taxation or any requirement connected therewith which is other or more burdensome," while paragraph 2 specifies that a tax "shall not be less favorably levied." Regardless of these differences in language, only differences in tax treatment that materially disadvantage the foreign person relative to the domestic person are properly the subject of the Article.

☐☐☐g☐☐☐☐☐☐

Paragraph 1 provides that a national of one Contracting State may not be subject to taxation or connected requirements in the other Contracting State that are different from, or more burdensome than, the taxes and connected requirements imposed upon a national of that other Contracting State in the same circumstances. As noted above, whether or not the two persons are both taxable on worldwide income is a significant circumstance for this purpose. The 1992 revision of the OECD Model added, after the words "in the same circumstances," the phrase "in particular with respect to residence," reflecting the fact that under most countries' laws residents are taxable on worldwide income and nonresidents are not. Since in the United States nonresident citizens are also taxable on worldwide income the Convention, like the U.S. Model, expands the phrase to refer, not to residence, but to taxation on worldwide income.

A national of a Contracting State is afforded protection under this paragraph even if the national is not a resident of either Contracting State. Thus, a U.S. citizen who is resident in a third country is entitled, under this paragraph, to the same treatment in Japan as a citizen of Japan who is in similar circumstances (i.e., who is resident in a third State). The term "national" in relation to a Contracting State is defined in subparagraph 1(j) of Article 3. The term includes both individuals and juridical persons.

☐☐☐g☐☐☐☐☐

Paragraph 2 of the Article, like the comparable paragraphs in the U.S. and OECD Models, provides that a Contracting State may not tax a permanent establishment of an enterprise of the other Contracting State less favorably than an enterprise of that first-mentioned State that is carrying on the same activities.

The fact that a U.S. permanent establishment of an enterprise of Japan is subject to U.S. tax only on income that is attributable to the permanent establishment, while a U.S. corporation engaged in the same activities is taxable on its worldwide income is not, in itself, a sufficient difference to deny national treatment to the permanent establishment. There are cases, however, where the two enterprises would not be similarly situated and differences in treatment may be warranted. For instance, it would not be a violation of the non-discrimination protection of paragraph 2 to require the foreign enterprise to provide information in a reasonable manner that may be different from the information requirements imposed on a resident enterprise, because information may not be as readily available to the Internal Revenue Service from a foreign as from a domestic enterprise. Similarly, it would not be a violation of paragraph 2 to impose penalties on persons who fail to comply with such a requirement (see, *e.g.*, sections 874(a) and 882(c)(2)). Further, a determination that income and expenses have been attributed or allocated to a permanent establishment in conformity with the principles of Article 7 (Business Profits) implies that the attribution or allocation was not discriminatory.

Section 1446 of the Code imposes on any partnership with income that is effectively connected with a U.S. trade or business the obligation to withhold tax on amounts allocable to a foreign partner. In the context of the Convention, this obligation applies with respect to a share of the partnership income of a partner resident in Japan, and attributable to a U.S. permanent establishment. There is no similar obligation with respect to the distributive shares of U.S. resident partners. It is understood, however, that this distinction is not a form of discrimination within the meaning of paragraph 2 of the Article. No distinction is made between U.S. and non-U.S. partnerships, since the law requires that partnerships of both U.S. and non-U.S. domicile withhold tax in respect of the partnership shares of non-U.S. partners. Furthermore, in distinguishing between U.S. and non-U.S. partners, the requirement to withhold on the non-U.S. but not the U.S. partner's share is not discriminatory taxation, but, like other withholding on nonresident aliens, is merely a reasonable method for the collection of tax from persons who are not continually present in the United States, and as to whom it otherwise may be difficult for the United States to enforce its tax jurisdiction. If tax has been over-withheld, the partner can, as in other cases of over-withholding, file for a refund.

Paragraph 2 also provides that a Contracting State is not obligated under this paragraph to grant to a resident of the other Contracting State any personal allowances, reliefs, and reductions for tax purposes that it grants to its own residents on account of their civil status or family responsibilities. Thus, if a sole proprietor who is a resident of Japan has a permanent establishment in the United States, in assessing income tax on the profits attributable to the permanent establishment, the United States is not obligated to allow to the resident of Japan the personal allowances for himself and his family that he would be permitted to take if the permanent establishment were a sole proprietorship owned and operated by a U.S. resident, despite the fact that the individual income tax rates would apply.

Paragraph 3 prohibits discrimination in the allowance of deductions. When a resident of a Contracting State pays interest, royalties or other disbursements to a resident of the other Contracting State, the first-mentioned Contracting State must allow a deduction for those payments in computing the taxable profits of the resident as if the payment had been made under the same conditions to a resident of the first-mentioned Contracting State. Paragraph 3, however, does not require a Contracting State to give non-residents more favorable treatment than it gives to its own residents. Consequently, a Contracting State does not have to allow non-residents a deduction for items that are not deductible under its domestic law (for example, expenses of a capital nature).

The term "other disbursements" is understood to include a reasonable allocation of executive and general administrative expenses, research and development expenses and other expenses incurred for the benefit of a group of related persons that includes the person incurring the expense.

The opening part of the paragraph lists provisions of the Convention where the protection it gives for deductions does not apply. These are concerned with transactions involving potential abuse, where it is appropriate for the Contracting States to continue to apply their anti-avoidance safeguards. The paragraph carves out from its coverage the special relationship paragraphs at paragraph 8 of Article 11 (Interest), paragraph 4 of Article 12 (Royalties) and paragraph 3 of Article 21 (Other Income). Neither State is forced to apply the non-discrimination principle in such cases. The exception with respect to paragraph 8 of Article 11 would include the denial or deferral of certain interest deductions under Code section 163(j).

Paragraph 3 also provides that any debts of a resident or enterprise of a Contracting State to a resident of the other Contracting State are deductible in the first-mentioned Contracting State for computing the taxable capital of the resident under the same conditions as if the debt had been contracted to a resident of the first-mentioned Contracting State. Even though, for general purposes, the Convention covers only income taxes, under paragraph 6 of this Article, the nondiscrimination provisions apply to all taxes levied in both Contracting States, at all levels of government. Thus, this provision may be relevant for both Contracting States as it would apply to property taxes imposed at the local level.

Paragraph 4 requires that a Contracting State not impose more burdensome taxation or connected requirements on an enterprise of that Contracting State that is wholly or partly owned or controlled, directly or indirectly, by one or more residents of the other Contracting State than the taxation or connected requirements that it imposes on other similar enterprises of that first-mentioned Contracting State. For this purpose it is understood that "similar" refers to similar activities or ownership of the enterprise.

This rule, like all non-discrimination provisions, does not prohibit differing treatment of entities that are in differing circumstances. Rather, a protected enterprise is only required to be treated in the same manner as other enterprises that, from the point of view of the application of the tax law, are in substantially similar circumstances both in law and in fact. The taxation of a distributing corporation under section 367(e) on an applicable distribution to foreign shareholders does not violate paragraph 4 of the Article because a foreign-owned corporation is not similar to a domestically-owned corporation that is accorded nonrecognition treatment under sections 337 and 355.

For the reasons given above in connection with the discussion of paragraph 2 of the Article, it is also understood that the provision in section 1446 of the Code for withholding of tax on non-U.S. partners does not violate paragraph 4 of the Article.

It is further understood that the ineligibility of a U.S. corporation with nonresident alien shareholders to make an election to be an "S" corporation does not violate paragraph 4 of the Article. If a corporation elects to be an S corporation (requiring 75 or fewer shareholders), it is generally not subject to income tax and the shareholders take into account their pro rata shares of the corporation's items of income, loss, deduction or credit. (The purpose of the provision is to allow an individual or small group of individuals to conduct business in corporate form while paying taxes at individual rates as if the business were conducted directly.) A nonresident alien does not pay U.S. tax on a net basis, and, thus, does not generally take into account items of loss, deduction or credit. Thus, the S corporation provisions do not exclude corporations with nonresident alien shareholders because such shareholders are foreign, but only because they are not net-basis taxpayers. Similarly, the provisions exclude corporations with other types of shareholders where the purpose of the provisions cannot be fulfilled or their mechanics implemented. For example, corporations with corporate shareholders are excluded because the purpose of the provision to permit individuals to conduct a business in corporate form at individual tax rates would not be furthered by their inclusion.

□□□□*g*□□□□□□

Paragraph 5 of the Article confirms that no provision of the Article will prevent either Contracting State from imposing the branch-level taxes described in paragraph 9 of Article 10 (Dividends) and paragraph 10 of Article 11 (Interest).

□□□□*g*□□□□□□

As noted above, notwithstanding the specification in Article 2 (Taxes Covered) and subparagraph (d) of paragraph 1 of Article 3 (General Definitions) of taxes covered by the Convention for general purposes, for purposes of providing non-discrimination protection this Article applies to taxes of every kind and description imposed by a Contracting State or a political subdivision or local authority thereof. Customs duties are not considered to be taxes for this purpose.

□*e*□□□□□□□□□□ □□*e*□□□□□□□*e*□□

Article 24 is not subject to the saving clause of subparagraph 4(a) of Article 1 (General Scope) by virtue of the exceptions in paragraph 5 of that Article. Thus, for example, a U.S. citizen who is a resident of Japan may claim benefits in the United States under this Article.

Nationals of a Contracting State may claim the benefits of paragraph 1 regardless of whether they are entitled to benefits under Article 22 (Limitation on Benefits), because that paragraph applies to nationals and not residents. They may not claim the benefits of the other paragraphs of this Article with respect to an item of income unless they are generally entitled to treaty benefits with respect to that income under a provision of Article 22.

Article 25 (Mutual Agreement Procedure)

This article provides the mechanism for taxpayers to bring to the attention of the competent authorities of the Contracting States issues and problems that may arise under the Convention. This article also provides a mechanism for cooperation between the competent authorities of the Contracting States to resolve disputes and clarify issues that may arise under the Convention and to resolve cases of double taxation not provided for in the Convention. The competent authorities of the two Contracting States are identified in subparagraph (k) of paragraph 1 of Article 3 (General Definitions).

□□□g□□□□□

Paragraph 1 provides that where a person considers that the actions of one or both Contracting States will result in taxation that is not in accordance with the Convention he may present his case to the competent authority of the Contracting State of which he is a resident or, if his case comes under paragraph 1 of Article 24, a national.

Although the typical cases brought under this paragraph will involve economic double taxation arising from transfer pricing adjustments, the scope of this paragraph is not limited to such cases. For example, if the United States treats income derived by a company resident in Japan as attributable to a permanent establishment in the United States, and the Japanese resident believes that the income is not attributable to a permanent establishment, or that no permanent establishment exists, the Japanese company may bring a complaint under paragraph 1 to the competent authority of Japan.

It is not necessary for a person bringing a complaint first to have exhausted the remedies provided under the national laws of the Contracting States before presenting a case to the competent authorities. However, unlike the U.S. Model, but like the OECD Model, paragraph 1 provides that a case must be presented to a competent authority within three years from the first notification of the action giving rise to taxation not in accordance with the provisions of the Convention. For example, if the taxpayer were notified by Japan on June 15, 2007 of a transfer pricing adjustment, the taxpayer could present the case to the U.S. competent authority at any time before June 15, 2010.

Paragraph 18 of the Commentary to Article 25 of the OECD Model states that identifying the date of the first notification, as referred to in paragraph 1, should be done in the manner most favorable to the taxpayer. For example, if an action results from the tax authority following a published procedure, the first notification would not be the date of publication of the procedure, but rather the date on which the taxpayer was first notified of the decision to apply the procedure to him.

Paragraph 2 addresses the manner in which the competent authorities will deal with cases brought by taxpayers under paragraph 1. Paragraph 2 provides that if the competent authority of the Contracting State to which the case is presented judges the case to have merit, and cannot reach a unilateral solution, it shall seek an agreement with the competent authority of the other Contracting State pursuant to which taxation not in accordance with the Convention will be avoided.

Any agreement is to be implemented even if such implementation otherwise would be barred by the statute of limitations or by some other procedural limitation, such as a closing agreement. Paragraph 2, however, does not prevent the application of domestic-law procedural limitations that give effect to the agreement (*e.g.*, a domestic-law requirement that the taxpayer file a return reflecting the agreement within one year of the date of the agreement).

Where the taxpayer has entered a closing agreement (or other written settlement) with the United States before bringing a case to the competent authorities, the U.S. competent authority will endeavor only to obtain a correlative adjustment from Japan. □*ee* Rev. Proc. 2002-52, 2002-31 I.R.B. 242, § 7.04. Because, as specified in paragraph 2 of Article 1 (General Scope), the Convention cannot operate to increase a taxpayer's liability, temporal or other procedural limitations can be overridden only for the purpose of making refunds and not to impose additional tax.

Paragraph 3 authorizes the competent authorities to resolve difficulties or doubts that may arise as to the application or interpretation of the Convention. The paragraph includes a non-exhaustive list of examples of the kinds of matters about which the competent authorities may reach agreement. This list is purely illustrative; it does not grant any authority that is not implicitly present as a result of the introductory sentence of paragraph 3.

The competent authorities may, for example, agree to the same allocation of income, deductions, credits or allowances between an enterprise in one Contracting State and its permanent establishment in the other (subparagraph (a)) or between related persons (subparagraph (b)). These allocations are to be made in accordance with the arm's length principle underlying Article 7 (Business Profits) and Article 9 (Associated Enterprises). Agreements reached under these subparagraphs may include agreement on a methodology for determining an appropriate transfer price, common treatment of a taxpayer's cost sharing arrangement, or upon an acceptable range of results under that methodology.

As indicated in subparagraph (c), the competent authorities also may agree to settle a variety of conflicting applications of the Convention. They may agree to settle conflicts regarding the characterization of particular items of income (clause (i) of subparagraph (c)), the characterization of persons (clause (ii)), the application of same source rules to particular items of income (clause (iii)), and to meaning the of a term (clause (iv)). They also may agree as to advance pricing arrangements (subparagraph (d)).

Since the list under paragraph 3 is not exhaustive, the competent authorities may reach agreement on issues not enumerated in paragraph 3 if necessary to avoid double taxation. For example, the competent authorities may seek agreement on a uniform set of standards for the use of exchange rates, or agree on consistent timing of gain recognition with respect to a transaction to the extent necessary to avoid double taxation. Agreements reached by the competent authorities under paragraph 3 need not conform to the internal law provisions of either Contracting State.

Finally, paragraph 3 authorizes the competent authorities to consult for the purpose of eliminating double taxation in cases not provided for in the Convention and to resolve any difficulties or doubts arising as to the interpretation or application of the Convention. This provision is intended to permit the competent authorities to implement the treaty in particular cases in a manner that is consistent with its expressed general purposes. It permits the competent authorities to deal with cases that are within the spirit of the provisions but that are not specifically covered. An example of such a case might be double taxation arising from a transfer pricing adjustment between two permanent establishments of a third-country resident, one in the United States and one in Japan. Since no resident of a Contracting State is involved in the case, the Convention does not apply, but the competent authorities nevertheless may use the authority of the Convention to prevent the double taxation of income.

⬚⬚⬚*g*⬚⬚⬚⬚⬚

Paragraph 4 provides that the competent authorities may communicate with each other directly for the purpose of reaching an agreement. This makes clear that the competent authorities of the two Contracting States may communicate without going through diplomatic channels. Such communication may be in various forms, including, where appropriate, through face-to-face meetings of the competent authorities or their representatives.

⬚*e*⬚⬚⬚*e*⬚⬚⬚*e*⬚⬚*e*⬚⬚⬚⬚*e*⬚⬚⬚⬚⬚⬚⬚⬚⬚*e*⬚⬚⬚⬚⬚⬚⬚⬚⬚⬚*e*⬚*e*⬚⬚⬚⬚⬚⬚⬚⬚⬚⬚⬚⬚*e*⬚*e*⬚⬚⬚⬚⬚⬚⬚⬚

A case may be raised by a taxpayer under a treaty with respect to a year for which a treaty was in force after the treaty has been terminated. In such a case, the ability of the competent authorities to act is limited. They may not exchange confidential information, nor may they reach a solution that varies from that specified in their respective domestic laws.

A case also may be brought to a competent authority under a treaty that is in force, but with respect to a year prior to the entry into force of the treaty. The scope of the competent authorities to address such a case is not constrained by the fact that the treaty was not in force when the transactions at issue occurred, and the competent authorities have available to them the full range of remedies afforded under this article.

⬚⬚⬚⬚*g*⬚⬚⬚⬚⬚⬚ *e* *e*⬚⬚⬚⬚⬚⬚⬚⬚⬚⬚⬚⬚⬚⬚

International tax cases may involve more than two taxing jurisdictions (*e.g.*, transactions among a parent corporation resident in country A and its subsidiaries resident in countries B and

C). As long as there is a complete network of treaties among the three countries, it should be possible, under the full combination of bilateral authorities, for the competent authorities of the three Contracting States to work together on a three-sided solution. Although country A may not be able to give information received under Article 26 (Exchange of Information) from country B to the authorities of country C, if the competent authorities of the three countries are working together, it should be possible, given the bilateral relationships between each of the countries, for them to arrange for the authorities of country B to give the necessary information directly to the tax authorities of country C, as well as to those of country A. Each bilateral part of the trilateral solution must, of course, not exceed the scope of the authority of the competent authorities under the relevant bilateral treaty.

Relationship to other Articles

Article 25 is not subject to the saving clause of subparagraph 4(a) of Article 1 (General Scope) by virtue of the exceptions in paragraph 5 of that Article. Thus, rules, definitions, procedures, etc. that are agreed upon by the competent authorities under this Article may be applied by the United States with respect to its citizens and residents even if they differ from the comparable Code provisions. Similarly, as indicated above, U.S. law may be overridden to provide refunds of tax to a U.S. citizen or resident under this Article.

A person may seek relief under Article 25 regardless of whether he is generally entitled to benefits under Article 22 (Limitation on Benefits). As in all other cases, the competent authority is vested with the discretion to decide whether the claim for relief is justified.

Article 26 (Exchange of Information)

Paragraph 1

Paragraph 1 provides for the exchange of information between the competent authorities of the Contracting States. The information to be exchanged is that which is relevant to carrying out the provisions of the Convention or the domestic laws of the United States or Japan concerning taxes of every kind imposed by a Contracting State. Consistent with the U.S. Model, exchange of information applies with respect to all taxes imposed at the national level, and thus applies to a broader category of taxes than those referred to in Article 2 (Taxes Covered) or subparagraph (d) of paragraph 1 of Article (3) (General Definitions). This is confirmed by paragraph 5 of Article 26.

Exchange of information with respect to each Contracting State's domestic tax law is authorized insofar as the taxation under domestic tax law is not contrary to the Convention. Thus, for example, information may be exchanged even if the transaction to which the information relates is a purely domestic transaction in the requesting Contracting State and, therefore, the exchange is not made to carry out the Convention. An example of such a case is provided in the OECD Commentary: a company resident in the United States and a company resident in Japan transact business between themselves through a third-country resident company. Neither Contracting State has a treaty with the third state. To enforce their internal laws with respect to transactions of their residents with the third-country company (since there is no relevant treaty in force), the Contracting States may exchange information regarding the prices that their residents paid in their transactions with the third-country resident.

Unlike the U.S. Model, but like the OECD Model, paragraph 1 does not include an illustrative list of matters to which information subject to the exchange of information may relate. The U.S. Model provides that the competent authorities shall exchange such information as is relevant for carrying out domestic laws of the Contracting States, "including information related to the assessment or collection of, the enforcement or prosecution in respect of, or the determination of appeals in relation to," the relevant taxes. The omission of this illustrative language is not intended restrict the matters with respect to which information may be exchanged. Thus, the competent authorities may request and provide information for tax cases under examination or criminal investigation, in collection, on appeals, or under prosecution. This result is reinforced by paragraph 2, which provides that the information exchanged may be disclosed to persons or authorities "involved in the assessment or collection of, the enforcement or prosecution in respect of, or the determination of appeals in relation to," the relevant taxes.

Paragraph 1 states that information exchange is not restricted by Article 1 (General Scope). Accordingly, information may be requested and provided under this article with respect to persons who are not residents of either Contracting State. For example, if a third-country resident has a permanent establishment in Japan, which engages in transactions with a U.S. enterprise, the United States could request information with respect to that permanent establishment, even though the third-country resident is not a resident of either Contracting State. Similarly, if a third-country resident maintains a bank account in Japan, and the Internal Revenue Service has reason to believe that funds in that account should have been reported for U.S. tax purposes but have not been so reported, information can be requested from Japan with respect to that person's account, even though that person is not the taxpayer under examination.

Paragraph 1 also provides that the requesting Contracting State may specify the form in which information is to be provided so that the information can be usable in the judicial proceedings of the requesting Contracting State. In this regard, unlike the U.S. Model, paragraph 1 does not explicitly authorize the use of depositions of witnesses to obtain information under this article.

The article authorizes the competent authorities to exchange information on a routine basis, on request in relation to a specific case, or spontaneously. It is contemplated that the Contracting States will utilize this authority to engage in all of these forms of information exchange, as appropriate.

□□□□*g*□□□□□□

Paragraph 2 provides that any information exchanged will be treated as secret, subject to the same disclosure constraints as information obtained under the laws of the requesting Contracting State. Paragraph 2 further provides that information received may be disclosed only to persons, including courts and administrative bodies, involved in the assessment, collection, or administration of, the enforcement or prosecution in respect of, or the determination of the of appeals in relation to, the taxes referred to in paragraph 1, or to supervisory bodies. The information received may be disclosed to such persons, authorities or supervisory bodies only to the extent necessary for them to perform their respective responsibilities, and such persons, authorities or supervisory bodies shall use the information only for purposes of discharging their responsibilities. Information received may be disclosed in public court proceedings or in judicial decisions.

Pursuant to paragraph 6 of the Notes, it is understood that the term "authorities . . . involved in the administration of" taxes includes authorities, such as the Office of Chief Counsel for the Internal Revenue Service, that provide legal advice to governmental entities that are directly involved in the activities described in paragraph 2 of Article 26. Paragraph 7 of the Notes sets out the understanding that the term "supervisory bodies" includes authorities that supervise the general administration of the government of a Contracting State. Thus, information may be disclosed to legislative bodies, such as the tax-writing committees of Congress and the General Accounting Office, engaged in the oversight of the activities described in paragraph 2 of Article 26. Information received by these bodies must be for use in the performance of their role in overseeing the administration of U.S. tax laws.

□□□*g*□□□□□

Paragraph 3 provides that the obligations undertaken in paragraphs 1 and 2 to exchange information do not require a Contracting State to carry out administrative measures that are at variance with the laws or administrative practice of either Contracting State. Nor is a Contracting State required to supply information not obtainable under the laws or administrative practice of either Contracting State, or to disclose trade secrets or other information, the disclosure of which would be contrary to public policy.

Thus, a requesting Contracting State may be denied information from the other Contracting State if the information would be obtained pursuant to procedures or measures that are broader than those available in the requesting Contracting State. However, each Contracting State has confirmed in paragraph 8 of the Notes its ability to obtain and exchange certain information under Article 26. The information that may be obtained and exchanged includes information held by financial institutions, nominees, or persons acting in an agency or fiduciary capacity (but does not include information relating to communications between a legal representative in its role as such and its client to the extent that the communications are protected under the domestic law of the requested Contracting State). In the case of the United States, the scope of the privilege for such confidential communications is coextensive with the attorney-client privilege under U.S. law. The Contracting States may also obtain and exchange information relating to the ownership of legal persons.

While paragraph 3 states conditions under which a Contracting State is not obligated to comply with a request from the other Contracting State for information, the requested State is not precluded from providing such information, and may, at its discretion, do so subject to the limitations of its internal law.

Paragraph 4 provides that, in order to effectuate the exchange of information as provided in paragraph 1, each Contracting State shall take necessary measures to ensure that its competent authority has sufficient powers under its domestic law to obtain information for the exchange of information regardless of whether that Contracting State may need such information for purposes of its own tax. This paragraph thus reaches the same result as the second sentence of paragraph 3 of Article 26 of the U.S. Model. The competent authority of the United States has the power to obtain information for the exchange of information pursuant to a tax treaty regardless of whether the United States has a domestic tax interest in such information. A change in the domestic law of Japan in 2003 has allowed Japan to agree to this paragraph by similarly providing the competent authority of Japan with the power to obtain information for the exchange of information pursuant to a tax treaty regardless of whether Japan has a domestic tax interest in such information.

As noted above in the discussion of paragraph 1, paragraph 5 confirms that Article 26 applies to taxes of every kind and description imposed by a Contracting State, and thus is not limited to the taxes referred to in Article 2 (Taxes Covered) or subparagraph (d) of paragraph 1 of Article (3) (General Definitions), insofar as the taxation thereunder is not contrary to the provisions of the Convention.

A tax administration may seek information with respect to a year for which a treaty was in force after the treaty has been terminated. In such a case the ability of the other tax administration to act is limited. The treaty no longer provides authority for the tax administrations to exchange confidential information. They may only exchange information pursuant to domestic law.

The competent authority also may seek information under a treaty that is in force, but with respect to a year prior to the entry into force of the treaty. The scope of the competent authorities to address such a case is not constrained by the fact that a treaty was not in force when the transactions at issue occurred, and the competent authorities have available to them the full range of information exchange provisions afforded under this Article. Even though a prior treaty may have been in effect during the years in which the transaction at issue occurred, the exchange of information provisions of the current treaty apply.

Article 27 (Administrative Assistance)

Paragraph 1 provides for assistance in collection of taxes to the extent necessary to ensure that treaty benefits are enjoyed only by persons entitled to those benefits under the terms of the Convention. Under paragraph 1, a Contracting State will endeavor to collect on behalf of the other Contracting State only those amounts necessary to ensure that any exemption or reduced rate of tax at source granted under the Convention by that other Contracting State is not enjoyed by persons not entitled to those benefits. For example, if the payer of a U.S.-source portfolio dividend receives a Form W-8BEN or other appropriate documentation from the payee, the withholding agent is permitted to withhold at the portfolio dividend rate of 10 percent. If, however, the addressee is merely acting as a nominee on behalf of a third-country resident, paragraph 1 would obligate Japan to take collection action against a person for the difference in applicable withholding rates in response to a specific request from the U.S. competent authority. □□□*g*□□□□□□

Paragraph 2 makes clear that the provisions of paragraph 1 do not obligate the Contracting State asked to collect the tax to carry out administrative measures that are different from those used in the collection of its own taxes, or that would be contrary to its sovereignty, security or public policy, in the process of providing such assistance.

Article 28 (Diplomatic Agents and Consular Officers)

This Article confirms that any fiscal privileges to which members of diplomatic missions or consular posts are entitled under general provisions of international law or under special agreements will apply notwithstanding any provisions to the contrary in the Convention. The agreements referred to include any bilateral agreements, such as consular conventions, that affect the taxation of diplomats and consular officials and any multilateral agreements dealing with these issues, such as the Vienna Convention on Diplomatic Relations and the Vienna Convention on Consular Relations. The U.S. generally adheres to the latter because its terms are consistent with customary international law.

The Article does not independently provide any benefits to diplomatic agents and consular officers. Article 18 (Government Service) does so, as do Code section 893 and a number of bilateral and multilateral agreements. In the event that there is a conflict between the Convention and international law or such other treaties, under which the diplomatic agent or consular official is entitled to greater benefits under the latter, the latter laws or agreements shall have precedence. Conversely, if the Convention confers a greater benefit than another agreement, the affected person could claim the benefit of the tax treaty.

Article 28 is not subject to the saving clause of subparagraph 4(a) of Article 1 (General Scope) by virtue of the exceptions in paragraph 5 of that Article. Thus, the benefits of Article 28 will be provided by each Contracting State to its residents and, in the case of the United States, its citizens. While this coordination between the saving clause and Article 28 technically differs from the coordination in the U.S. Model, in almost all cases the result will be the same. Pursuant to paragraph 5(b) of Article 1 of the U.S. Model, Article 28 of the U.S. Model is not subject to the saving clause only to the extent benefits would be granted to a resident of the United States who is neither a citizen of United States nor a person who has been admitted for permanent residence there. Members of diplomatic missions or consular posts of Japan, however, are very unlikely to be or become citizens of the United States or persons admitted for permanent residence there. Therefore, in almost all case the result under the Convention will be the same as the result under the U.S. Model.

Article 29 (Consultations)

Article 29 establishes a procedure that may be followed by the Contracting States in the event that one of the Contracting States considers that a substantial change in the domestic laws of the other Contracting State relevant to the Convention has been made. In such a case, the first-mentioned Contracting State may make a request to the Contracting State making the change in law for consultations with a view to determining the possible effect of such change on the balance of benefits provided by the Convention and, if appropriate, to amending the provisions of the Convention to arrive at an appropriate balance of benefits. This provision is intended to provide a procedure in a case where changes to the law of one of the Contracting States may alter significantly the legal application of the Convention as intended by the Contracting States as of the date of signature. In the event that these consultations lead to an agreement regarding amendments to the Convention, any such amendments would, of course, require a protocol or new treaty which would be subject in the United States to Senate advice and consent to ratification.

The request for consultations must be in writing, and as a communication from one Contracting State to the other should be made through diplomatic channels. The requested Contracting State shall enter into consultations with the Contracting State making the request within three months of the date of receipt of the request.

Article 30 (Entry into Force)

This Article contains the rules for bringing the Convention into force and giving effect to its provisions.

□□□□*g*□□□□□□□

Paragraph 1 provides that the Convention is subject to ratification and that the instruments of ratification shall be exchanged as soon as possible.

In the United States, the process leading to ratification and exchange of the instruments of ratification is as follows. Once a treaty has been signed by authorized representatives of the two Contracting States, the Department of State sends the treaty to the President who formally transmits it to the Senate for its advice and consent to ratification, which requires approval by two-thirds of the Senators present and voting. Prior to this vote, however, it generally has been the practice for the Senate Committee on Foreign Relations to hold hearings on the treaty and to make a recommendation regarding its approval to the full Senate. Both Government and private sector witnesses may testify at these hearings. After receiving the Senate's advice and consent to ratification, the treaty is returned to the President for his signature on the ratification document. The President's signature on the document completes the process in the United States. Upon completion of the process, the United States may exchange the instruments of ratification.

Paragraph 1 also provides that the Convention shall enter into force on the date of the exchange of instruments of ratification. The date on which a treaty enters into force is not necessarily the date on which its provisions take effect. Rules that determine when the provisions of the treaty will have effect are provided in paragraph 2.

☐☐☐*g*☐☐☐☐☐☐

Paragraph 2 provides rules that determine when the Convention is applicable in Japan and in the United States to withholding taxes and to other taxes.

The rules with respect to Japanese taxes are contained in paragraph 2(a). Under paragraph 2(a)(i), the Convention shall be applicable in Japan with respect to taxes withheld at source (principally the Articles covering dividends, interest and royalties) for amounts taxable on or after July 1 of the calendar year in which the Convention enters into force if the Convention enters into force before April 1 of a calendar year and for amounts taxable on or after January 1 of the year following the year in which the Convention enters into force if the Convention enters into force after March 31 of a calendar year. For example, if the instruments of ratification are exchanged and the treaty enters into force on June 30 of a given year, the withholding rates specified in paragraph 2 and 3 of Article 10 (Dividends) would be applicable in Japan to any dividends taxable on or after January 1 of the following year. This two-part rule allows the benefits of the withholding reductions to be put into effect as soon as possible. The delay to July 1 or January 1, as the case may be, is required to allow sufficient time for withholding agents to be informed about and prepare for the change in withholding rates.

Under paragraph 2(a)(ii), the Convention shall be applicable in Japan with respect to income taxes not withheld at source and the enterprise tax for income for any taxable year beginning on or after January 1 of the year following the year the Convention enters into force.

The rules with respect to U.S. taxes are contained in paragraph 2(b). Under paragraph 2(b)(i), the Convention shall be applicable in the United States with respect to taxes withheld at source for amounts paid or credited on or after July 1 of the calendar year in which the Convention enters into force if the Convention enters into force before April 1 of a calendar year and for amounts paid or credited on or after January 1 of the year following the year in which the Convention enters into force if the Convention enters into force after March 31 of a calendar year. For example, if the instruments of ratification are exchanged and the treaty enters into force on June 30 of a given year, the withholding rates specified in paragraph 2 and 3 of Article 10 (Dividends) would be applicable in the United States to any dividends paid or credited on or after January 1 of the following year. As noted above with respect to Japanese withholding taxes, this two-part rule allows the benefits of the withholding reductions to be put into effect as soon as possible. If for some reason a withholding agent withholds U.S. tax at a higher rate than that provided by the Convention (perhaps because it was not able to re-program its computers before the payment is made), a beneficial owner of the income that is a resident of Japan may make a claim for refund pursuant to section 1464 of the Code.

Under paragraph 2(b)(ii), the Convention shall be applicable in the United States with respect to taxes other than those withheld at source (including the excise tax on insurance premiums and the branch profits tax) for taxable periods beginning on or after January 1 of the year following the date on which the Convention enters into force.

Paragraph 3 provides an exception to the entry into force of this Convention and the termination of the prior Convention. The treatment under Articles 19 (Teachers and Researchers) and 20 (Students and Trainees) of the prior Convention may be more generous than the treatment under the corresponding articles of the Convention. Certain individuals covered by those Articles may have made their plans to visit the host State upon the assumption that Article 19 or 20 of the prior Convention would apply to them. Paragraph 3 ensures that the rules do not change with respect to such individuals. It provides that an individual who is entitled to the benefits of Article 19 or 20 of the prior Convention at the time of entry into force of this Convention shall continue to be entitled to such benefits as if the prior Convention had remained in force. This additional grandfather rule is necessary because there are circumstances in which the twelve-month grace period of paragraph 4 would not cover the entire period at issue.

Paragraph 4 provides that the prior Convention generally ceases to have effect with respect to any tax as of the date this Convention takes effect with respect to that tax under paragraphs 1 and 2. As in many recent U.S. treaties, however, paragraph 4 also provides an exception to this general rule. Under paragraph 4, if any person entitled to benefits under the prior Convention would have been entitled to greater benefits than under this Convention, the prior Convention shall, at the election of such person, continue to have effect in its entirety for a twelve-month period from the date on which this Convention otherwise would have had effect under paragraph 2.

Thus, a taxpayer may elect to extend the benefits of the prior Convention for one year from the date on which the provisions of the new Convention would first take effect. During the period in which the election is in effect, the provisions of the prior Convention will continue to apply only insofar as they applied before the entry into force of the Convention. If the grace period is elected, all of the provisions of the prior Convention must be applied for that additional year. The taxpayer may not apply certain, more favorable provisions of the prior Convention and, at the same time, apply other, more favorable provisions of this Convention. The taxpayer must choose one treaty or the other.

For example, suppose the instruments of ratification are exchanged on June 30, 2004 and the Convention thus enters into force on that date. The new Convention would take effect with respect to taxes withheld at source for amounts paid or credited on or after January 1, 2005. If the election under paragraph 4 is made, the provisions of the prior Convention regarding withholding would continue to have effect for amounts paid or credited at any time prior to January 1, 2006. The provisions of the Convention regarding withholding (including the rules of Article 22 (Limitation on Benefits)) would have effect for amounts paid or credited on or after January 1, 2006. If the election is made with respect to other U.S. taxes, the Convention would be applicable for taxable periods beginning on or after January 1, 2006. In the absence of such an election, the Convention would be applicable for taxable periods beginning on or after January 1, 2005.

The prior Convention shall terminate on the last date on which it has effect with respect to any tax in accordance with the provisions of this paragraph 4.

Article 31 (Termination)

The Convention is to remain in force until terminated by one of the Contracting States in accordance with the provisions of Article 31. Under this article, either Contracting State may terminate the Convention after five years after entry into force; such termination would be accomplished by giving six months written notice of termination through the diplomatic channel.

If such notice of termination is given, the provisions of the Convention with respect to taxes withheld at source will cease to have effect for amounts taxable, in the case of Japan, or paid or credited, in the case of the United States, on or after January 1 of the year following the expiration of the six-month period. With respect to other taxes, the effective date of termination mirrors the rules with respect to entry into force. That is, the Convention will cease to have effect in Japan for income for any taxable year beginning on or after January 1 of the year following the expiration of the six-month period and will cease to have effect in the United States for taxable periods beginning on or after January 1 of the year following the expiration of the six-month period.

Article 31 relates only to unilateral termination of the Convention by a Contracting State. Nothing in that Article should be construed as preventing the Contracting States from concluding a new bilateral agreement, subject to ratification, that supersedes, amends or terminates provisions of the Convention without the six-month notification period and earlier than five years after the date the Convention enters into force.

Customary international law observed by the United States and other countries, as reflected in the Vienna Convention on Treaties, allows termination by one Contracting State at any time in the event of a "material breach" of the agreement by the other Contracting State.

Understanding of the Negotiators

The Convention between the Government of Japan and the Government of the United States for the Avoidance of Double Taxation and the Prevention of Fiscal Evasion with respect to Taxes on Income, signed on November 6, 2003, contains rules allocating taxing jurisdiction over salaries, wages and other similar remuneration between Japan and the United States. The provisions of paragraph 10 of the Protocol to the Convention address the treatment under the Convention of employees benefiting from "stock option plans." Paragraph 10 includes a rule that allocates taxing jurisdiction over the benefits enjoyed by employees under stock option plans relating to the period between grant and exercise of an option between the two countries in order to avoid double taxation. In cases where double taxation nevertheless may arise because of the interaction of the domestic tax rules of Japan and the United States, paragraph 10 further provides that the competent authorities will endeavor to resolve any difficulties or doubts by way of mutual agreement with the aim of ensuring no unrelieved double taxation.

The interaction between the domestic taxation rules regarding the treatment of stock options in Japan and the United States can be complex. The rules of the Convention, in particular the rule included in paragraph 10 of the Protocol, that allocate taxing jurisdiction may not be enough to avoid double taxation in all cases. The purpose of this Understanding is to establish a framework by which double taxation can be avoided to the maximum extent possible as provided for in paragraph 10.

The tax treatment in each country of stock options provided to employees is similar to that in the other country. Generally, in each country the tax treatment depends on whether stock options meet specified requirements and conditions and therefore are considered so-called "qualified" stock options. The recipient of qualified stock options is not taxed at grant or on exercise of the option. Instead, the recipient is taxed only on sale of the stock. The recipient of "nonqualified" stock options generally is taxed on exercise of the option and on sale of the stock.

There are some differences between the tax treatment in each country of stock options provided to employees. For example, in Japan nonresidents generally would be subject to tax under its domestic tax law on the gain from sales of stock acquired through the exercise of stock options qualified in Japan. In the United States nonresidents (other than U.S. citizens) generally would not be subject to tax on the gain from sales of stock acquired through the exercise of qualified stock options even if they had been residents at the time of grant or exercise.

Article 14 of the Convention allocates taxing jurisdiction with respect to salaries, wages and other similar remuneration derived by a resident of one country in respect of an employment by providing generally that the other country (the "source" country) may tax such income if the employment is exercised in such source country and certain other conditions are met. Paragraph 10 of the Protocol provides that the benefits enjoyed by employees under stock option plans relating to the period between grant and exercise of an option are regarded as "other similar remuneration" for the purposes of Article 14.

Paragraph 10 of the Protocol further provides that the source country may tax only that proportion of such benefits which relates to the period or periods between the grant and the exercise of the option during which the individual has exercised the employment in that source country. Neither Article 14 nor paragraph 10 of the Protocol provides rules regarding when or in what manner the source country may tax such income. The source country may tax such income or may choose to forego taxation of such income in some or all circumstances. For example, Japan as the source country may tax such income upon the sale of the stock acquired through the exercise of a qualified stock option, and the United States as the source country may tax such income earned by non-resident citizens without resort to subparagraph (a) of paragraph 4 of Article 1. The limitations in Article 13 on the taxation of gains on the sale of stock by nonresidents are not relevant to the taxation of such income because paragraph 10 of the Protocol provides that such income is regarded as "other similar remuneration" for the purposes of Article 14. Under Article 23, any tax imposed by the source country on a resident of the other country on such income in accordance with the Convention, including Article 14 and paragraph 10 of the Protocol, shall be allowed as a credit against the tax imposed on that resident by the country of residence, subject generally to domestic law limitations on the foreign tax credit in the country of residence (as discussed below).

Our detailed discussions related to the treatment of stock options under the Convention were aided by consideration of the fact patterns in the attached Annex. In many cases, the rules in the Convention, in particular the rule included in paragraph 10 of the Protocol, that allocate taxing jurisdiction between Japan and the United States, in combination with the domestic law foreign tax credit provisions of Japan and the United States, operate to eliminate any potential for double taxation. For example, the rules in the Convention that allocate taxing jurisdiction, in combination with the domestic law foreign tax credit provisions, eliminate any potential for double taxation in the cases in which stock options are treated consistently by both the tax law of Japan and the tax law of the United States either as nonqualified stock options or as qualified stock options

In the remaining cases, the domestic law foreign tax credit provisions of Japan and the United States and the rules in the Convention, in particular the rule included in paragraph 10 of the Protocol, that allocate taxing jurisdiction between Japan and the United States may not operate to completely alleviate double taxation. In these cases, while Article 14 and paragraph 10 of the Protocol allow the source country to tax certain income and Article 23 obligates the country of residence to allow such tax as a credit against the tax imposed on that resident by the country of residence, the limitations in the domestic law foreign tax credit provisions (such as limitations related to carryforward or carryback periods and limitations related to differences in the characterization of items of income or gain) operate in a manner that may prevent the alleviation of double taxation in cases where the treatment of the stock options under the domestic tax law of one country is different than the treatment in the other country. With respect to these cases, pursuant to paragraph 10 of the Protocol, the competent authorities of Japan and the United States will, through a mutual agreement procedure, provide measures for the elimination of double taxation at the time of sale of the underlying stock, including the allowance of a foreign tax credit for taxes paid to the source country at the time of exercise or sale that are imposed in accordance with Article 14 and paragraph 10 of the Protocol. The limitations in the domestic law foreign tax credit provisions of Japan and the United States will not prevent the alleviation of double taxation in these cases due to the provision of measures for the elimination of double taxation by the competent authorities through the mutual agreement procedure. Thus, the provision of measures for the elimination of double taxation, including a foreign tax credit, by the competent authorities through the mutual agreement procedure in these cases will eliminate any potential for double taxation.

There may be other cases relating to stock options that raise double taxation issues. In these other cases, the competent authorities of Japan and the United States, as provided for in paragraph 10 of the Protocol, will explore ways to reach appropriate agreement through the mutual agreement procedure on a case-by-case basis with the aim of ensuring no unrelieved double taxation.

Masatsugu Asakawa
Director, International Tax Policy Division
Ministry of Finance
Japan

Date: 2003年 11 月 6 日

Barbara M. Angus
International Tax Counsel
Department of the Treasury
United States of America

Date: November 6, 2003

These fact patterns were developed to aid the discussion related to the treatment of stock options under the Convention.

Each fact pattern below is based on the following common facts:

- A stock option with a price of option 15, which is equal to the value of the stock, is granted to an employee.
- The employee exercises the option in 5 year, acquiring the stock for 15. At the time of exercise, the value of the stock is 20.
- The employee sells the stock for 40 in a subsequent year.
- The employee is a resident of, and performs services in, either Japan or the United States throughout the period between grant and exercise.
- The employee is a resident of either Japan or the United States in the year the stock option is exercised and in the year the stock is sold.

Fact pattern 1. The employee is a resident of Japan in the year of exercise and the year of sale. The period between grant and exercise is five years; the employee is a resident of, and performs services in, the United States for four of those years and Japan for one of those years.

Fact pattern 2. The employee is a resident of the United States in the year of exercise and the year of sale. The period between grant and exercise is five years; the employee is a resident of, and performs services in, Japan for four of those years and the United States for one of those years.

Fact pattern 3. The employee is a resident of Japan in the year of exercise and a resident of the United States in the year of sale. The period between grant and exercise is five years; the employee is a resident of, and performs services in, the United States for four of those years and Japan for one of those years.

Fact pattern 4. The employee is a resident of the United States in the year of exercise and a resident of Japan in the year of sale. The period between grant and exercise is five years; the employee is a resident of, and performs services in, Japan for four of those years and the United States for one of those years.

There are four alternatives under each fact pattern, resulting in 16 possible general cases. In the first alternative, the stock option is regarded as nonqualified under the tax laws of both the United States and Japan. In the second alternative, the stock option is regarded as qualified under the tax laws of both the United States and Japan. In the third alternative, the stock option is regarded as nonqualified under the tax law of the United States, but is regarded as qualified under the tax law of Japan. In the fourth alternative, the stock option is regarded as nonqualified under the tax law of Japan, but is regarded as qualified under the tax law of the United States.

In cases resulting from the first and second alternatives, the rules in the Convention, in particular the rule included in paragraph 10 of the Protocol, that allocate taxing jurisdiction between Japan and the United States, in combination with the domestic law foreign tax credit provisions of Japan and the United States, operate to eliminate any potential for double taxation.

In some of the cases resulting from the third and fourth alternatives the rules in the Convention, in particular the rule included in paragraph 10 of the Protocol, that allocate taxing jurisdiction between Japan and the United States, in combination with the domestic law foreign tax credit provisions of Japan and the United States, also operate to eliminate any potential for double taxation. However, in the remaining cases, the domestic law foreign tax credit provisions of Japan and the United States (including limitations related to carryforward or carryback periods and limitations related to differences in the characterization of items of income or gain) and the rules in the Convention, in particular the rule included in paragraph 10 of the Protocol, that allocate taxing jurisdiction between Japan and the United States may not operate to completely alleviate double taxation. With respect to these cases, pursuant to paragraph 10 of the Protocol, the competent authorities of Japan and the United States will, through a mutual agreement procedure, provide measures for the elimination of double taxation at the time of sale of the underlying stock, including the allowance of a foreign tax credit for taxes paid to the source country at the time of exercise or sale that are imposed in accordance with Article 14 and paragraph 10 of the Protocol.